The Pragmatics of Public Communication

R. R. Allen
The University of Wisconsin

Ray E. McKerrow
The University of Maine

Charles E. Merrill Publishing Company
A Bell & Howell Company
Columbus Toronto London Sydney

Published by
Charles E. Merrill Publishing Company
A Bell & Howell Company
Columbus, Ohio 43216

This book was set in Caledonia and Futura Book.
The Production Editor was Sharon Thomason.
The cover was prepared by Will Chenoweth.
Cover photograph courtesy of Linda Briscoe.

International Standard Book Number: 0–675–08487–3

Library of Congress Catalog Card Number: 76–49286

Photo Credits

Chapter 1	Laima Druskis/Editorial Photocolor Archives
Chapter 2	Bruce Anspach/Editorial Photocolor Archives
Chapter 3	Bernstein Photos
Chapter 4	Raimondo Borea ASMP/Editorial Photocolor Archives
Chapter 5	Daniel S. Brody/Editorial Photocolor Archives
Chapter 6	Daniel S. Brody/Editorial Photocolor Archives
Chapter 7	Bruce Anspach/Editorial Photocolor Archives
Page 131	Courtesy Wadsworth Publishing Company, Inc.

2 3 4 5 6 7—83 82 81 80 79 78 77

Printed in the United States of America

To JoAnne and Gayle

Contents

Preface

The Pragmatics of Public Communication is intended for college-level courses in which primary attention is given to the development of basic public-speaking competencies. Since students come to such courses in search of practical skills rather than theoretical knowledge, this book avoids the presentation of theory for the sake of theory. It is unashamedly pragmatic. An attempt is made to include only that information that has direct application to skill development.

This textbook is based on a number of assumptions about learning. First, it is assumed that students learn basic skills most easily when the goals of instruction are clearly identified. Consequently, instructional objectives are presented in each chapter. These objectives provide the basis for teacher-student dialectic regarding learning expectations. Second, it is assumed that basic student creative and evaluative skills are encouraged through the use of principles and examples. Thus, an attempt has been made to present principles in a clear way, offering examples, whenever possible, against which the student may test each principle in action. Third, it is assumed that students learn better through active participation than through passive reception. Therefore, structured learning experiences are built into each chapter to encourage active student involvement. Fourth, it is assumed that basic public communication skills should unfold gradually and systematically. To this end, learning activities for each content area progress from recall and comprehension through application to the higher cognitive processes of analysis and syntheses. Students are not expected to demonstrate highly complex speech skills before they have perfected requisite behaviors.

The Pragmatics of Public Communication is a flexible instructional resource. Its most obvious use is in classroom settings designed to promote experiential learning and peer-group interaction. When used in this way, the instructor may assign chapter sections to be read outside of class. Answers to the concept verification exercises may be collected at the beginning of each class period for which reading was assigned to verify that students have mastered the material at recall and comprehension levels. During class periods, students may work in small groups on concept utilization exercises, coming together for whole-class discussions when small-group work has been completed. Major synthesis activities, especially speeches, would normally be completed individually outside of class for later presentation to the whole class or subgroups thereof.

This book also may be used in settings designed to encourage individualized study and in accelerated classroom settings. Students pursuing a course of independent study may complete all of the structured learning experiences at their convenience, meeting with the instructor only to discuss problems and progress and to orally present speeches. In the accelerated classroom, the instructor may require out-of-class completion of the majority of the structured learning activities in order that class time might be devoted to theoretical extensions of knowledge.

In preparing this book, the authors have been reminded of the debt owed to others. We are especially grateful to the generations of University of Wisconsin teaching assistants in Communication Arts 105 who watched this book gradually evolve from a syllabus and a loose assortment of materials into a more carefully articulated instructional resource. They will notice, we suspect, that at times, we have treasured their ideas as our own. We are also indebted to Linda Whipp and Pat Anderson whose careful working of the learning activities is reflected in the *professional supplement,* which accompanies this text. We owe a note of appreciation to numerous former students whose rhetorical flourishes are found as examples in these pages and to the 1976 Summer Session Communication Arts 101 class for suffering through this book in mimeographed edition. Finally, the authors acknowledge the helpful criticisms of Richard Johannesen, Jim Hughey, and David Axon and the expert editorial assistance of Sharon Thomason of the Charles E. Merrill staff.

R. R. Allen

Ray E. McKerrow

The Pragmatics of Public Communication

1

the study of public communication

learning objectives

By the conclusion of this chapter you will be able to:

1. Identify five assumptions about the learning of communication skills.

2. Match each of the five assumptions with descriptions of those assumptions.

3. Identify the assumption that is violated in sample learning instances.

4. Identify the four dimensions of public communication competence that are stressed in this book.

5. Match the four dimensions of competence with descriptions of those dimensions.

6. Identify the three main forces that influence rhetorical choices.

7. Match the three forces that influence rhetorical choice with descriptions of those forces.

8. Identify the dimension of competence that is inadequately employed in sample speaking situations.

9. Identify the rhetorical force being violated in sample speaking situations.

In a sense, a teacher makes a contract with his students. The students agree to pay a certain sum in return for certain skills and knowledge. But, most of the time, they are expected to pay for something that is never carefully defined or described. They are asked to buy (with effort) a product they are not allowed to see and that is only vaguely described. The teacher who doesn't clearly specify his instructional objectives, who doesn't describe how he intends the learner to be different after his instruction, is clearly taking advantage of his students.[1]

Robert F. Mager

Education is a funny sort of business. In almost every other business both the consumer and the proprietor approach a transaction with reasonably clear, shared expectations. Mary's parents and Mary's orthodontist both expect proper occlusion and a winning smile when Mary's teeth are no longer laced with wires. In education, however, the product of the transaction is not as clearly defined or depicted. Both teachers and students often begin their transactions with vague and widely disparate notions about what each hopes to accomplish.

In the headnote to this chapter, Mager maintains that the relationship between a teacher and a student should be a contractual one. As in any contract, expectations should be established at the outset, and both parties should accept the responsibility for fulfilling their parts of the agreement.

This chapter focuses on the expectations that teachers and students may share in a course in public communication. On completion of the chapter, you should have a clear notion of both the methods and the general goals that are relevant to the pragmatic study of public communication.

Learning in Pragmatic Perspective

Although there is nothing wrong with knowing something for the sheer joy of knowing it, most students are not enrolled in a basic course in public communication primarily to enhance their knowledge of the principles and theories of public discourse. Rather, they have chosen the course, or have had it chosen for them, in order to improve their communication skills in public settings.

We have used the word *pragmatic* to emphasize the practical nature of this book. An attempt has been made to exclude information that is not directly related to your development of public speaking competencies.

The preparation of this book has been based on the five assumptions about learning that are described below.

Students Learn Best When They Understand Instructional Goals

A noted educational psychologist once talked about his own experiences as a teacher at a major university. Early in his career he taught as he was taught: he lectured; he tested; and he assigned course grades that approximated the bell-shaped curve (mostly *Cs*, fewer *Bs* and *Ds*, in roughly equivalent proportions, and even fewer *As* and *Fs*, also in equivalent proportions). Then one day he decided to tell his students what he wanted them to learn. What happened? They learned! Feeling guilty for awarding so many *As* and *Bs* and so few *Ds* and *Fs*, he decided to increase his course expectations while continuing to inform his students of his new and more difficult instructional goals. What happened? His students continued to meet his expectations even though his standards had been substantially elevated.

On the assumption that students are more likely to attain learning goals when those goals are made known, each chapter of this book begins by specifying the particular behaviors that the chapter is designed to promote. As you consider each chapter, you may wish to discuss these goals with your instructor to ensure that your expectations coincide.

Precepts and Examples Contribute to Student Skill Development

When learning skills, either basic physical skills or complex cognitive skills, students profit both from precepts or principles, which provide guidelines for their improvement, and from examples, which demonstrate how the principle works in practice. For example, if you wished to learn to serve a tennis ball with speed and accuracy, you would profit from precepts or principles that describe the form most likely to produce the desired results. You would also profit from the viewing of films or videotapes that show tennis players properly, and even improperly, following these guidelines.

In the chapters that follow, essential principles for public communication are presented. In most instances, examples are also provided in order that you may test the validity of the principle by observing it in action. At the end of each section of each chapter, you will find questions, labelled verification, designed to test your basic recall and comprehension of the principles presented in that section.

Student Skills Are Best Acquired through Active Involvement

In many college courses, instructors assume the active role while students sit by in relative passivity. Small wonder that many young teachers have observed, "I never really understood that concept until I tried to teach it." We learn best when we place ourselves in dynamic confrontation with ideas.

Even in public communication courses, teachers often play the active role while relegating students to passive roles. Thus, the instructor talks and hopes that the student will make the transition from hearing lectures to making speeches without active involvement in-between.

This book is ideally suited for courses in which students are actively involved in learning during each class session. The instructor is best viewed as the facilitator of student learning. At the end of each section of each chapter you will find learning activities, labeled utilization, that require you to use principles as guidelines for your own critical and creative involvement in public communication.

Public Communication Skills Should Unfold Gradually

Public communication skills are complex skills. They must be nurtured in a gradual and systematic way. The driver education instructor would be ill-advised to give the car keys to his or her charges with the advice, "Take a few turns up and down the turnpike, and come back, if you can, and we'll talk about it." Similarly, the teacher of public communication is ill-advised to invite the student to "solo" before he or she has acquired the skills that invite success rather than failure.

This book provides for the gradual unfolding of public communication competencies. Each section of each chapter invites you to grow from concept recall, through concept comprehension, to concept application, analysis, and synthesis. Within each chapter, lower-order learning activities precede higher-order activities. The learning of individual behaviors is provided for before you are asked to put it all together as you demonstrate complex behaviors. Similarly, the chapters are sequentially organized. You will begin by perfecting skills of delivery, language use, and organization before you are expected to develop and demonstrate skills related to informative, persuasive, and ceremonial speaking. You will not be asked to give speeches before you have been taught the requisite skills. So relax. When it is time to speak, you will be ready.

Students Have Much to Learn from Each Other

In many college courses, students are placed in competition with each other. In the pragmatically oriented public communication course, students learn from each other as they grow in communication skills. As you work through the learning activities provided in the book, you will have occasion to test your ideas against those of your peers in cooperative undertakings. When you present informative, persuasive, or ceremonial speeches, it will be your peers whom you seek to influence. You will learn to trust and appreciate classmates who are honest, open, and constructive in criticism. You will learn that the collective wisdom of your peers is a valuable supplement to the informed judgment of your instructor.

In the process of learning and growing together, you will establish relationships with peers that are unusual in traditional classroom settings. You will know more of your classmates by name and will value their reactions to your messages.

As we have mentioned, this textbook actively enlists your involvement in learning communication skills. You are about to begin working through the first set of exercises. Each exercise is matched with one of the objectives at the beginning of this chapter. As you work through each exercise, reflect on the particular objective the exercise seeks to accomplish. The concept verification questions are designed merely to ensure that you have grasped the material presented in the preceding pages. The concept utilization questions ask you to extend your knowledge by applying it to new examples, instances, or situations. You should now pause to consider the major ideas that were presented in the preceding pages. As you work through each exercise, look back only if absolutely necessary to complete the task.

EXERCISES

VERIFICATION

1. Complete the following five assumptions about the learning of communication skills.

   a. Students learn best when they understand ______________________________
   ________________.

b. P____________ and e____________ contribute to student skill development.

c. Students skills are best acquired through a____________ i____________.

d. Public communication skills should u____________ g____________.

e. Students have much to ____________.

VERIFICATION

2. Match the letter preceding each assumption (in question 1) with the description of that assumption.

a. _____ Complex skills should be taught a little bit at a time.

b. _____ Knowing objectives facilitates learning.

c. _____ Participation enhances skill acquisition.

d. _____ Generalizations and illustrations can provide guidelines for development of skills.

e. _____ Peer criticism can be a valuable source of information.

UTILIZATION

3. Identify the assumption being violated in each of the sample learning instances provided below. Use each assumption once.

a. You're preparing for a mid-term examination and you realize you have no idea what's going to be on it.

b. You ask a student if he or she wants to study with you for an upcoming examination. He or she responds with "Forget it; why should I help you?"

c. On the first day of class, the teacher announces, "Tomorrow you will present an informative speech."

d. The typing instructor lectures for three days on the location of the keys on the keyboard and then asks you to type a page.

e. A father stays up all night on Christmas Eve trying to assemble the Jim Dandy Road Racing set for his young child because the instructions look like they were written for an engineer.

Public Communication in Pragmatic Perspective

The previous section considered some of the methods of instruction that are useful in teaching the practical skills of public speaking. This section will identify the kinds of skills that are important to public communication effectiveness.

The Dimensions of Public Communication Competence

Since the time of ancient Greece and Rome, teachers of rhetoric have organized instruction around the major dimensions of public speaking competence. The four dimensions emphasized in this book are delivery, language, organization, and invention.

Delivery. Delivery refers to the presentation of ideas through vocal and physical behavior. The effective speaker establishes a direct sense of communication with the audience through effective eye contact, facial expression, gesture, movement, and voice. Effective delivery seems to grow spontaneously out of the ideas being advanced. It gives the impression that the speaker is genuinely interested in winning an appropriate response from the audience. It conveys a sense of personal involvement of a speaker with a message in dynamic interplay with an audience. As you establish personal goals for this course, the perfection of delivery skills should be numbered among them. Chapter 2 identifies specific objectives that will guide your development of appropriate delivery behaviors.

Language. In informal conversation most people pay little attention to language choices; ideas and words are born in a flash of spontaneous expression. In public communication contexts, however, speakers are much more careful in choosing the language through which their ideas are expressed. Public speakers must express ideas in clear, appropriate, and vivid language. In chapter 3, you will perfect precise skills of language usage for public contexts. If this instruction succeeds, sometime during this term someone will step up to you and say, "Nicely expressed," or "Gee, I wish I'd have said that."

Organization. A public speech is a fleeting phenomenon. In a conversation, a listener may stop a speaker to request clarification. When reading an essay, a reader may reread and reread until the writer's meaning is clear. In a speech, however, the communication must be understandable at the moment of utterance, or it is lost forever. Chapter 4 will identify specific learning objectives that will enable you to structure your messages in a clear and understandable way. The skills of organization that this chapter seeks to develop will be of value to you in both written and oral communication.

Invention. Classically, invention taught ways of discovering (places to look for) arguments or strategies of content. In this text the discovery of ideas will be considered in terms of the major purposes that public messages are intended to serve. Chapter 5 considers the means through which information is communicated. Chapter 6 considers the means through which audiences are persuaded to accept a speaker's point of view. Chapter 7 considers the means through which a speaker satisfies the requirements of ceremonial occasions. In each of these chapters, specific learning goals are identified that will help you to discover ways of satisfying your communicative purposes.

Forces that Influence Rhetorical Choices

The dimensions of rhetorical choice are exercised in public contexts. As you approach the study of public communication, it is important that you consider the larger forces that govern the specific choices that you will make.

Personal integrity. Any rhetorical choice that is made reflects your personal sense of integrity. Audiences are not always well informed; they can be lied to with remarkable ease (as our experience with public revelations about the activities of former presidents, the CIA, and the FBI have all too clearly demonstrated). The "end justifies the means" ethic, which dominated what is now known as "The Watergate Affair," maligned the integrity of otherwise respected men. Was it worth the cost?

As a speaker, you have responsibility for more than the presentation of ideas. If the audience accepts your program and the program fails, you shoulder a part of the blame. The "let the buyer beware" ethic of the commercial world should be rejected. In the marketplace of ideas, you as seller are obliged to follow the purchase through and to stand accountable for any failures that were, at the time the program was sold, within your power to comprehend and warn against.

Ultimately, the rhetorical choices you make as you create your messages reflect your personal ethics. That reflection may uphold or, in the face of accusation, destroy your reputation as an honest, forthright speaker. You should not mislead, misinterpret, or distort. Your research should be thorough, and your documentation should be accurate and explicit. You should reflect qualities of character worthy of respect. As Quintilian observed, the effective speaker is the *good* man speaking well.

Audience. What the audience expects you to provide is a crucial consideration as you develop your ideas. What the audience wants to hear may be vastly different from what you believe they should hear. The rhetorical problem is this: How do you phrase and present what you want to say in such a manner that an audience may attend, understand, believe, or empathize?

One answer is to sidestep the problem—tell the audience what they want to hear in the way that they want to hear it. This is ethically proper only if you also share the same values and beliefs as your audience.

Another approach is to adopt a position that is not in violent confrontation with your audience's viewpoints. President Ford, introducing the topic of amnesty at a Veterans of Foreign Wars convention, did face the issue. His solution was to reject unconditional amnesty, which the VFW was on record as opposing, in favor of "earned reentry" for draft evaders. In this manner, one hopes, the president maintained his personal integrity while winning audience acceptance.

The central concern in rhetorical decision making is to bring together the speaker's intent with the audience's expectations, values, and beliefs. This does not mean that you must mimic the audience's beliefs in every situation or assume a position more moderate than your belief. A tactic that differs from acquiesing to audience wishes or charting a less extreme course, as did Gerald Ford, is to stand your ground. By clearly indicating the discrepancy between your position and that of the audience and appealing for a fair hearing, you may at least gain audience attention. While your goal may fail, you may succeed in raising doubts where none existed. At the very least, you may win approval for your handling of a touchy rhetorical problem.

Occasion. In addition to your own sense of integrity and the expectations of the audience, rhetorical decisions are made against the background of occasions. In the case of ceremonial settings, as chapter 7 suggests, funerals, commemorative holidays, and other occasions place constraints on the choices that you make.

Audiences are sensitive to the requirements of occasions: one does not deprecate the accomplishments of the deceased at a funeral, nor does one violate the traditional themes of patriotism and sacrifice associated with Memorial Day or Independence Day celebrations. Additionally, your integrity is not exempt on such occasions. If you can't say anything good about the deceased, perhaps it is better to decline the invitation to speak than to compromise your principles to please the living. Similarly, if your views would shatter the sanctity of a national holiday, perhaps it would be better to seek some other time and place for the expression of your ideas.

In rhetorical settings, choices are not simply between this or that delivery, this or that language, this or that mode of organization, or this or that theme. Such decisions are always made in the context of what the particular, unique combination of speaker, audience, and occasion will allow, or even demand. The study of public communication is as much an art as it is a science. As you learn the dimensions of rhetorical choice available to you, you must also develop a sensitivity to what is right and appropriate and meaningful when speaking to different audiences on different occasions on different themes.

EXERCISES

VERIFICATION

4. List the four dimensions of public communication competence.

a.

b.

c.

d.

VERIFICATION

5. Match the four dimensions of competence with their descriptions.

a. ____________________ It is more important in speaking than in written discourse.

b. ____________________ Use of gestures is a part of this.

c. ____________________ One of its qualities is vividness.

d. ____________________ It has to do with choosing ideas to achieve rhetorical purposes.

VERIFICATION

5. List the three main forces that influence rhetorical choices.

a.

b.

c.

VERIFICATION

7. Match the three forces that influence rhetorical choices with their descriptions.

   a. ______________ The audience's wishes may be a critical influence.

   b. ______________ Your personal ethics are an important influence.

   c. ______________ The setting may influence rhetorical choices.

UTILIZATION

8. Identify the dimension of competence that is inadequately employed in the descriptions of speaker behavior provided below. Use each dimension only once.

   a. ______________ While moving to her left to make a point, the speaker's right toe strikes her left heel, and she is catapulted through a nearby wall.

   b. ______________ The student commencement speaker questions the quality of the education that she has received and charges the faculty with being ill-informed, incompetent, and irrelevant.

   c. ______________ A junior high school teacher tells her class, "Your behavior is abrasive, arrogant, and counterproductive to effective pedagogical transactions."

   d. ______________ After hearing a distinguished lecturer, four college students argue for four hours about what the speaker's major theme was.

UTILIZATION

9. Identify the rhetorical force being violated in each of the sample situations. Use each rhetorical force once.

   a. ______________ You have just been inducted into the Sports Hall of Fame after being passed over for several years. The speaker talks about how unfairly you have been treated. His remarks are embarrassing to you and to other members of the audience.

b. ____________________ You are interviewing for a job you really want to get. You are aware that the interviewer is looking for someone who will be tough and ruthless in order to increase production, and that your own approach is much different. He asks you: "How would you increase production?" You reply, "Drive, baby, drive."

c. ____________________ You are invited to address your hometown Kiwanis club. You respond: "No problem, I can use the same speech I gave in my public communications class. I won't have to change a thing."

Notes

1. Robert F. Mager, *Preparing Instructional Objectives* (San Francisco, Cal.: Fearon Publishers, 1962), p. 16.

2

delivery

learning objectives

Recall | Comprehension | Application | Analysis | Synthesis

By the conclusion of this chapter you will be able to:

1. Identify two environmental aspects that influence communication.

2. Match the two environmental aspects with descriptions of those aspects.

3. Rank in order physical descriptions according to the quality of communication environment produced.

4. Analyze the quality of the communication environment provided by different speech settings.

5. Adapt room arrangements and conditions to promote more effective communication.

6. Identify four facets of physical behavior related to delivery.

7. Match the four facets of physical behavior with descriptions of those facets.

8. Identify the facet of physical behavior violated in sample situations.

9. Analyze the physical behavior of speakers.

10. Use facial expression, eye contact, gesture, and bodily movement in specified communication situations.

11. Identify four facets of vocal delivery behavior.

12. Match the four facets of vocal behavior with descriptions of those facets.

13. Identify the facet of vocal behavior violated in specific instances.

14. Analyze the vocal behavior of speakers.

15. Use variety in loudness, pitch, quality, and rate in specified communication situations.

Recall Comprehension Application Analysis Synthesis

16. Demonstrate effective vocal and physical behavior when reading aloud in groups.

17. Demonstrate effective vocal and physical behavior when telling stories to the entire class.

Pleads he in earnest?—Look upon his face,
His eyes do drop no tears; his prayers are jest;
His words come from his mouth; ours, from our breast;
He prays but faintly, and would be denied;
We pray with heart and soul.

Shakespeare, *Richard II*

In Shakespeare's play, the Duchess of York questions her husband's sincerity by claiming that he neither looks nor acts the part of an earnest pleader. While words alone may convey ideas, our manner of presentation often communicates whether we are in jest or are sincere —whether we are interested in the ideas our words convey or are merely filling time.

The impact of our presentational manner is especially important in public contexts. Although your ordinary delivery behavior may work well for you in everyday interactions, consider the effect of these behaviors as you enter the public context. Sloppy, indistinct speech may be the norm when communicating with friends, but you court disaster in taking the same approach before a public audience.

This chapter focuses on three areas of study related to the delivery or presentation of ideas: perceiving environmental demands, using effective physical behavior, and using effective vocal behavior. Familiarity with these dimensions will enable you to adapt your delivery behavior to the requirements of particular speaking situations.

Perceiving Environmental Demands

Our attempts to communicate are affected by the physical setting in which they occur. When you walk into a dean's office, does the dean get up and offer you his or her big, comfy chair? Probably not, as the dean finds it easier to communicate when sitting behind the desk, and you either stand or take a seat in front of the desk. In this instance spatial distance and physical trappings are used to maintain a sense of authority desired by the dean in communicating with students.

In public communication contexts, environmental forces are no less significant. This section is concerned with the choices you make as you perceive the effects of various environments on the presentation of your speech. We will concentrate on two general aspects of the environment: physical arrangement and physical conditions.

Physical Arrangement

Physical arrangement refers to the location of objects in space. In some cases, you may have little or no control over the physical arrangement of chairs or tables in a classroom, banquet hall, or meeting room. In many classrooms and assembly halls, the chairs are prearranged or immovable. The setting consists of a podium from which the speaker faces rows of chairs, arranged either in consecutive semicircles or in a box-like configuration. When speaking in this setting, the normal communication pattern is like the pattern in figure 1.

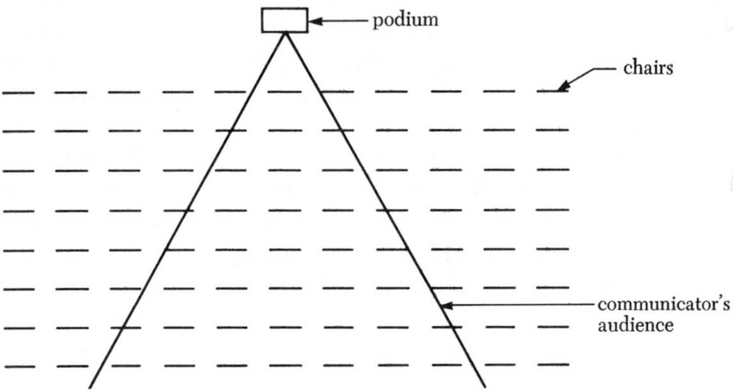

Figure 1

As the diagram illustrates, those directly in front of the speaker are automatically within direct contact. Those on the periphery are left out. By recognizing this, a speaker can adapt eye contact and physical movement to encompass a broader portion of the audience.

In many public communication contexts, physical arrangement may be altered with relative ease. For example, a public communication class was recently held in a room arranged as in figure 2.

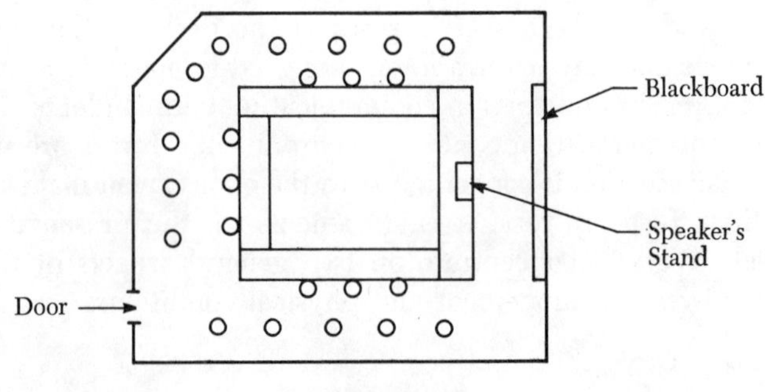

Figure 2

It was felt by the instructor that this arrangement was not particularly conducive to student speeches. The physical arrangement established two levels of audience involvement. Those seated at the tables were in close proximity to the speaker and thus were more likely to feel actively involved. However, the majority of the audience members were separated by great physical distance from the speaker. Additionally, it would be difficult for the speaker to maintain eye contact with audience members seated on his or her far left or right.

Given these shortcomings, three groups of students were asked to rearrange the furniture to promote better public communication. The three new arrangements are presented in figures 3, 4, and 5.

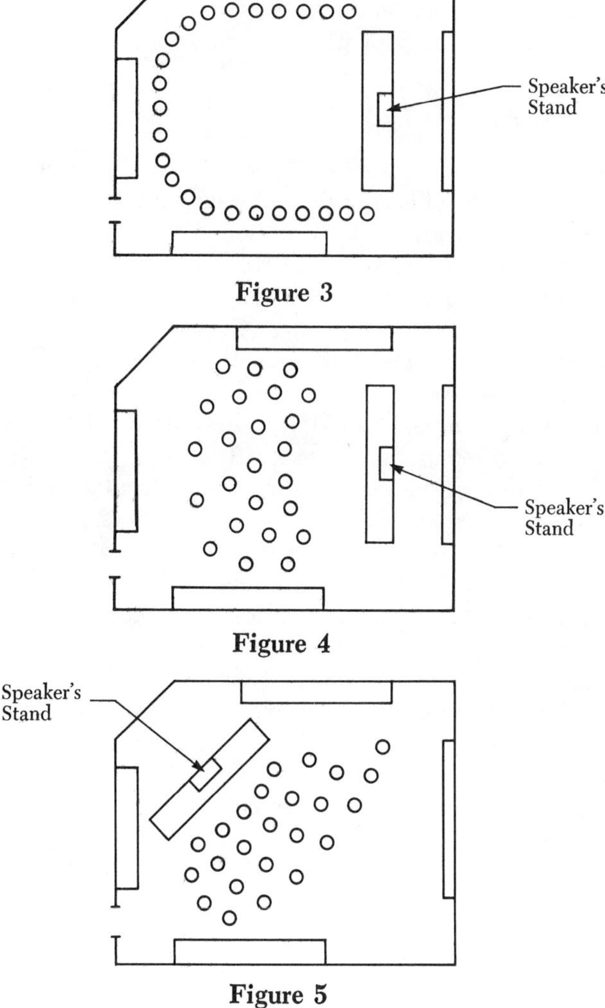

Figure 3

Figure 4

Figure 5

The arrangement in figure 3 does afford each audience member a clear view of the speaker. However, some audience members are still outside the speaker's normal line of vision. Additionally, student speakers using this arrangement reported that they felt on public display since they were so far removed from the audience. The arrangements in figures 4 and 5 were favorably evaluated by both speakers and audience members who experienced them. Both place audience members within the speaker's normal triangle of vision. They also provide a relatively unobstructed view of the speaker and provide environments in which the speaker does not feel physically divorced from his audience.

The possibilities for controlling the physical arrangement, or at least adapting to it, are endless. Insensitivity to matters of physical arrangement may interfere with your effectiveness.

Physical Conditions

In addition to being aware of physical arrangement, a speaker should attend to the effects of various physical conditions. Prior to delivering your speech, take time to consider the demands imposed by the size or shape of your room. If the room is massive and the distance between you and your audience is great, a casual, conversational, or "chatty" manner may be ineffective. On the other hand, if you and your audience are jammed into a small, stuffy, narrow banquet hall, overly powerful delivery may overwhelm the audience.

The constraints imposed by other physical conditions, such as hot, poorly ventilated rooms, noisy fans, or even hard, uncomfortable chairs, are also factors to consider in adjusting your presentation. If you plunge ahead without giving consideration to these factors, a sleepy audience may be inattentive, external noise may interfere with their ability to hear you, and prolonged physical discomfort may become more than they can bear—even if you possess the eloquence of a Churchill and the charisma of a John Kennedy.

Your response to these conditions may be to shorten your speech, project your voice more than you normally would, give the audience an opportunity to exercise before you begin, or adopt other methods of lessening the impact of the physical conditions. By displaying sensitivity to the demands of the environment, you may turn an otherwise odious experience into a pleasurable one for yourself and your audience.

EXERCISES

VERIFICATION

1. Identify the two environmental aspects that influence communication.

   a.

   b.

VERIFICATION

2. Match the two environmental aspects with their descriptions.

   a. ________________ Objects can be moved to affect distance or formality.

   b. ________________ Forces within a room may affect delivery.

UTILIZATION

3. Rank the descriptions of physical environment that follow in terms of the quality of communication environment produced (1–optimum, 2–fair, 3–poor).

   a. ____ The room is approximately ten feet by forty feet with seats jammed together to accommodate as many people as possible. The restaurant's kitchen is next door, and the dishwashing machine can be easily heard, as can the large fan that provides ventilation for the room.

   b. ____ The room is capable of seating fifty, with chairs spaced in a semicircle to accommodate about thirty-five people. The speaker can easily see all members of the audience. The room is well-lighted and ventilated; the chairs are cushioned.

   c. ____ The assembly hall is huge, with rows and rows of chairs stretching to the back of the room. Lighting is adequate, and the sound system is superb. Large supporting columns obstruct the speaker's view of some parts of the auditorium.

UTILIZATION

4. Do a thorough search of the class and lecture rooms in your building. Diagram the room that you think is most conducive to public communication and the room that you think is least conducive. Compare your diagrams with those produced by other students.

UTILIZATION

5. Working in groups of four or five, adapt your classroom, or a room assigned by the instructor, to render it most appropriate for speeches to be given to your class. Have all students in the class assume seats in your new arrangement. Have all members of your group speak briefly to the class from the rostrum to "experience" the new arrangement in action.

Using Effective Physical Behavior

The physical behavior of speakers makes a major contribution to their communicative effectiveness. Gestures, for example, can indicate size, number, or importance, while physical movement may mark transitions between ideas in a speech. Facial expressions may signal a speaker's sincerity or interest. In this section we will discuss the major dimensions of nonverbal communication: facial expression, eye contact, gestures, and bodily movement. As you examine each of these, consider their impact on the message you seek to deliver. Do the nonverbal cues supplement your messages and clarify your intent, or do they suggest a meaning or intent different than the one you wish to convey?

Facial Expressions

If you take pride in an ability to infer the mood of your friends by watching facial expressions, you are already familiar with this form of communication. A speaker can convey his or her distaste for a program by frowning, looking quizzical, or merely being unenthused. An explicit statement of disgust may not be necessary to communicate the feeling.

Unless you intend to express a meaning opposite from the words used, or say *more* with your face than with your words, your facial expression should match the feeling you wish to convey. Some years ago, several viewers were startled by President Johnson's countenance as he intoned the words "I come to you with a heavy heart." As he spoke, he seemed to be smiling and conveyed a feeling totally at odds with the thought being expressed. An otherwise enthusiastic speaker adopting a dour expression may give an audience cause to doubt the sincerity of his enthusiasm. A vibrant style, augmented by alive, happy facial expressions, may prove contagious. An audience may feel better just because the speaker feels good and conveys that feeling through his or her facial expression.

Eye Contact

An audience member, whether in a group of 10 people or 150 likes to feel involved in the speaking situation. A speaker who constantly looks away, or directs his or her gaze over the audience's heads, conveys to the listeners that their presence is unimportant.

While it is impossible to establish direct contact with every person in a large audience, speakers can direct their eyes to give the impression of looking at all members of the audience. By focusing on "happy faces" in selected portions of the audience, a speaker can convey to those persons and others in their vicinity that they are a part of his audience—that they are being communicated with. This can be done naturally without giving the visual impression of a "swivel-head." Focus on the left or right section of the audience for a while before establishing contact with another portion; in your haste to see them all you may see none of them individually.

By attending to audience members, a speaker can gain important clues about audience reaction to the message. Do they appear amused, befuddled, or possibly bored? If bored is the answer, perhaps a change in vocal or physical behavior will regain their attention and arouse their interest once more.

If you are speaking from memory or without notes or manuscript, it is fairly easy to maintain constant contact with the audience. On most occasions, however, you will use brief notes or a manuscript, and will find it necessary to break contact to consult your notes or to guard against losing your place in the written speech. Many speakers err by burying their heads in their notes. All the audience sees is a furrowed brow or the top of a head as the speaker concentrates on reading. A few cautions are in order. First, make certain the notes, or manuscript, are legible and readable so that a quick glance will suffice. Second, know the material well enough that you need not be literally tied to your notes. Finally, just as you wish to avoid becoming a "swivel-head," you will also wish to avoid conveying the image of an "apple-bobber" as you shift back and forth between notes and audience. Having readable notes and knowing what you want to say will help overcome this problem.

Gestures

In the heyday of the "elocutionists," speakers were trained in elaborate schemes of gesturing designed to evoke emotions in the audience. The remnants of this heritage may be observed in those few contemporary speakers who plan gestures and, in delivering their speeches, resemble robots. The artificiality of such planning can be overcome simply by gesturing in a spontaneous manner.

Descriptive gestures aid in illustrating physical dimensions. Indicating that two objects are two feet apart can be clarified by physically depicting the distance; telling someone how large an object is can also be depicted by showing the relative size through the use of your hands.

Implicative gestures, on the other hand, imply feelings or attitudes. They may act as *symbols* of particular attitudes. A clenched fist salute symbolizes an attitude of protest; a "V" sign made with your fingers may indicate either victory or peace. "Thumbs down" implies rejection; suddenly throwing your hands in the air may imply resignation or unbounded glee.

Whether describing objects or implying attitudes, gestures can enliven your discourse, enhance meaning, and help maintain audience interest. Although they may be used alone to communicate meaning, in public settings they are more often used as companions to the verbal message.

Bodily Movement

Some speakers deliver their messages with all the vigor and vitality of a concrete statue. They plant their feet firmly, grip the podium securely, fix a glassy stare on the audience, and launch their speech. At some point, the audience becomes more engrossed in watching knuckles whiten than in attending to the ideas being presented. At the other extreme, some speakers' state of constant motion—flailing away with arms and hands, pacing back and forth, moving erratically from side to side—causes the audience to become transfixed by the constancy of motion and to lose track of the message.

Obviously, we recommend that you adopt a middle course between these extremes, being neither immovable nor constantly in motion. Physical movement should be purposive; it should supplement and support the message being delivered. For example, you might move toward your audience, or lean toward the podium to convey the urgency or significance of an idea. Backing away from an audience has the opposite effect; it breaks the association you have established between an idea and its significance. This latter movement suggests that you have finished with an important point—you are ready to relax tensions and let the audience ponder the ideas before you go on. Sideways movement may also signal important changes in the flow of your ideas. Coupled with phrases such as "on the other hand" or "the next point to be considered is," left or right movement effectively cues the audience to prepare for changes in the direction of a speech.

Properly used, physical movement can aid in your control of the drama of the moment; improperly used, it may relieve your own tension but may also divert attention from the substance of your message to your physical antics. A final caution—make sure that your whole body seems involved in the act of communication. Avoid random nonpurposeful movement of the extremities. Be a whole person communicating.

EXERCISES

VERIFICATION

6. Identify the four facets of physical behavior related to delivery.

   a.

   b.

   c.

   d.

VERIFICATION

7. Match the four facets of physical behavior with the descriptions that follow. (Caution: one of the descriptions does not apply.)

   a. ____________________ refers to total physical stance and activity.

   b. ____________________ includes apparel as a central feature.

   c. ____________________ may either describe or imply.

   d. ____________________ suggests personal concern for audience member.

   e. ____________________ demonstrates appropriate feeling regarding the ideas being expressed.

UTILIZATION

8. Identify the facet of physical behavior being inadequately employed in the following instances. (Caution: one of the items does not apply.)

   a. ____________________ Speaker seems breathless.

   b. ____________________ Speaker seems shifty and evasive.

c. ____________________ Speaker seems unemotional about subject.

d. ____________________ Speaker seems involved only from the waist up.

e. ____________________ Speaker fails to adequately indicate the shape of the object being described.

UTILIZATION

9. Analyze the physical delivery behavior of three classmates who are asked to describe their home towns in presentations before the class.

UTILIZATION

10. Working in small groups, complete the following learning activities.
    a. 1. Working in dyads, maintain constant eye contact with your partner while talking about courses being taken this term.
       2. Switching to triads involving new partners, talk about your high schools while maintaining eye contact with both other participants.
       3. In five-person groups, discuss summer employment; take turns standing and being "speaker." If as an audience member you feel ignored, raise your hand.
    b. Working in triads, have each member deliver the phrases that follow using suitable facial expression.
       1. I come to you with a heavy heart.
       2. I want to make this perfectly clear.
       3. I never answer iffy questions.
       4. Work is the curse of the drinking class.
       5. I may not be pretty, but I'm beautiful.
    c. Working in triads, describe objects or events through gesture alone such that your peers can identify which of the following objects is being described:
       1. a prehistoric beast
       2. a corn stalk
       3. a bread basket
       4. Adolf Hitler
       5. a clothes dryer
       6. a TV test pattern
       7. an apple with a bite out of it
    d. Working in triads, take turns using implicative gestures in such a way that your peers can identify the meanings that follow.
       1. Absolutely not.
       2. Give it to me.
       3. You're out of your mind.

4. Let me think about it.
5. It's beyond my grasp.
6. He's great.
7. But what are we going to do about it?
8. I've done everything I can.
9. They struck hard and fast.
10. It was soft and flabby.

e. 1. Draw a design made up of geometric figures. Working in triads, stand and describe your design using both language and physical behavior. Have peers recreate the geometric design on paper. You should stand four feet from your peers, but you may move backward and forward when you feel compelled to do so.
2. Next have each speaker stand eight feet from the audience (two peers) and describe another geometric design. Each speaker may move laterally but not backward and forward.
3. Discuss the experience. Criticize the stance, physical movement, gesture, eye contact, and facial expression of each speaker.

Using Effective Vocal Behavior

Impassioned, yet sincere, vocal expression adds vitality and energy to your ideas, but an indifferent delivery may turn an audience away and make the reception of your ideas difficult. This section presents four characteristics normally associated with effective vocal behavior. As you examine them, consider the ways in which each characteristic may aid in dramatizing your ideas.

Loudness

A loud voice results when air is expelled from the lungs with maximum force and intensity. Conversely, when little force or intensity is applied, the sounds produced are almost inaudible. Shouting "I love you" to your family as you drive off conveys one meaning; whispering the same words in another context may convey quite a different meaning. Whether shouting or whispering, variations in volume can be used to indicate urgency, exasperation, or a myriad of other emotions.

The appropriateness of a loud or a soft voice depends on two factors: room size and the need for vocal variety. In most speech settings, speakers can use a volume level similar to that used in everyday conversations. Most rooms are either small enough so that sound carries easily to all parts of the room, or are equipped with a sound system to assist the speaker in conveying the message without having to shout. When these conditions are not present, the volume must be raised so that those seated in the back of a room do not have to strain to hear the speaker. If the audience cannot hear, they cannot very well attend to the message.

Changes in volume also add vocal variety and may be useful in emphasizing certain ideas and in building to a climactic point within the speech. Changes in volume can also reflect transitions between ideas and can help the speaker maintain audience interest in the unfolding of his or her message.

Pitch

Pitch is determined by the frequency of vocal-cord vibrations. Because of physical differences in vocal-cord size, people possess widely varying pitch levels. Although your normal pitch level may be an alto, soprano, or bass, you can go up or down the musical scale to add vitality to your delivery. Monotonous speakers ignore both loudness and pitch changes, and convey uninvolvement or disinterest in the subject.

Pitch changes may serve to emphasize important ideas or to signal transitions in the speech. By controlling changes in both volume and pitch, you can communicate your sense of involvement in the task, or your commitment to the proposal or sentiment being expressed.

Quality

Each person possesses a unique voice quality determined by the physical shape of resonating cavities. Andy Devine comes immediately to mind in discussing uniqueness of voices; he used his gravel voice to advantage in countless western movies and television shows.

To some extent, you can alter your voice, disguising it as mimics or impressionists do. Variations may help break the monotony of delivery; they may also evoke a humorous reaction as you give your version of John Wayne confronting the villains. In some speech situations, variations in quality are essential to securing the response you desire. For example, the effective telling of jokes, children's stories, or even ghost stories demands that you assume the vocal qualities of one or more characters.

Rate

The rate of your delivery is determined by the *duration* of sound and by the number of *pauses* between sounds. Words can be spoken at a hurried, clipped pace, or they can be drawn out. The general rate of delivery selected by a speaker must be such that an audience can follow the ideas being presented. Beginning speakers, prompted by their nervousness, often hurry through a speech. As they gain experience, they find it easier to control the rate for rhetorical effect.

Given a comprehensible rate, a speaker needs to vary that rate to maintain audience interest. A lack of variation may lead to a metronomic type of delivery sure to lull an audience to sleep. The rate can be varied by speeding up or slowing down the delivery or by using pauses between ideas. The interplay of these factors is extremely helpful in stressing important points, creating dramatic effects, and in accenting the meaning being expressed.

As we leave the subject of delivery, there are a few final thoughts we wish to share with you. If you have been at all apprehensive or fearful about presenting ideas in public, remember that you have already given a number of small speeches.

Also, it is important to remember that all speakers, regardless of reputation or experience, have felt anxiety prior to speaking. If they didn't, their personal commitment to the task would be open to question. This natural anxiety can be a tremendous asset when brought under control. A totally calm speaker may be dull to listen to. As you grow in public communication skill and experience, you will learn to make prespeech anxieties work for you, rather than against you.

EXERCISES

VERIFICATION

11. List the four facets of vocal behavior.

    a.

    b.

    c.

    d.

VERIFICATION

12. Match the facets of vocal behavior with the appropriate description. (Caution: two of the descriptions do not apply.)

    a. ____________________ Sounds are enunciated clearly and distinctly.
    b. ____________________ The average pace is 120 words per minute.
    c. ____________________ Each person's voice is different.

d. ________________ Variations in volume affect meaning.
e. ________________ The sounds used are correct.
f. ________________ The normal range is two octaves.

UTILIZATION

13. Identify the facet of vocal behavior violated in each situation. If none is violated, write "none."

a. ________________ A speaker finishes delivering a 3000 word speech in 7 minutes, 34.8 seconds.
b. ________________ An oscilloscope monitoring a speaker's delivery reveals no change in inflection or tone.
c. ________________ A speaker, attempting to mimic John Wayne, ends up sounding more like Truman Capote.
d. ________________ A speaker utilizes pauses to signal changes in the direction of his speech.
e. ________________ Your eardrum has been broken by the person who answers your phone call.

UTILIZATION

14. Analyze the vocal behavior of three of your classmates who have been asked to describe their present living accommodations.

UTILIZATION

15. Working in small groups, complete the following activities.
   a. Working in triads, communicate the statements presented below using the *volume* appropriate to each situation.
      1. Telling a friend in a crowded room, "Your zipper's open."
      2. Telling your roommate, "If you don't stop drumming your fingers while I'm studying, I'm going to break your fingers at the knuckles."
      3. Asking a friend in the back row of a large auditorium/classroom, "Can you hear me now?"
   b. Working in triads, communicate the statements presented below using *pitch* levels and changes appropriate to each situation.
      1. A television sports commentator saying, "He's coming down the lane; his stride seems broken; he's up, up, up; he's over—eighteen feet and seven inches, a new, world pole-vault record."
      2. A television commentator, trying not to create panic, "We interrupt this program to bring you the following weather bulletin: a tornado warning has been issued for Philmore County. Proceed to shelter immediately. Multiple funnel clouds have been seen approaching this

area. I repeat: take shelter immediately. Tornadoes have been seen in Philmore County.

3. A local fair announcer saying, "You will notice the parachutist clutching the struts of the ancient biwing plane approaching from the south. He's away, down . . . down . . . down . . . down . . . he falls in free flight."

c. Working in triads, deliver the following statements using a *rate* appropriate to the meaning and underlying emotion:
   1. If I've told you once, I've told you a thousand times—stop that!
   2. It was a terrible shock to him—yes, a terrible shock.
   3. The pain shot through him like a bullet.
   4. The relentless pain gnawed on, sapping from him all strength to fight it.
   5. The water faucet dripped on endlessly into the night—drip-drip, drip-drop, drop-drip.
   6. The train came round the steep curve and continued to increase speed as it came down the straight stretch of track. Its wheels sounded clickety-clack.

d. Working in triads, imitate the vocal *qualities* of the people whose names follow. Continue to practice until the voices are clearly recognizable. Sample statements are provided, although you may wish to create your own.
   1. Peter Lorre: "I have played a bad man in many movies, but I am really just a pussycat."
   2. Lily Tomlin (as Ernestine): "One ringy-dingy, two ringy-dingy. Is this the party to whom I am speaking?"
   3. Howard Cosell: "This is Howard Cosell, speaking to you from Madison Square Garden, the internationally renowned haven of pugilistic extravaganzas."
   4. Mae West: "Hello, big boy. Come on up and see me sometime."
   5. Jim Nabors (as Gomer Pyle): "Golly, Sergeant Carter, I was just trying to be helpful. You're about the best sergeant anybody ever could be."
   6. Minnie Pearl: "Howdy, I'm just so glad to be here."
   7. John Wayne: "Hello, big fella. I just got bushwhacked at Deadman's Pass."
   8. Liza Minelli: "It's Liza with a z-z-z, not Lisa with an s-s-s."
   9. Jimmy Stewart: "It's a, it's very difficult to talk when you keep chewin' on your words."
   10. Lily Tomlin (as Edith Ann): "I got my pigtail caught in the pencil sharpener. Even my split ends have split ends. And that's the truth.

UTILIZATION

16. Working in triads, assign one person to each speaking part in the following dialogue. Rehearse it very carefully, paying close attention to both vocal and physical behavior. Practice it as if you were giving it before the class. One or more groups will be asked to present the following excerpt from Dr. Seuss's *Horton Hatches the Egg.*

NARRATOR:	Sighed Mayzie, a lazy bird hatching an egg;
MAYZIE:	"I'm tired and I'm bored And I've kinks in my leg From sitting, just sitting here day after day. It's *work!* How I hate it! I'd *much* rather play! I'd take a vacation, fly off for a rest If I could find *someone* to stay on my nest! If I could find someone, I'd fly away free. . . ."
NARRATOR:	Then Horton, the Elephant, passed by her tree.
MAYZIE:	"Hello!"
NARRATOR:	Called the lazy bird, smiling her best.
MAYZIE:	"You've nothing to do and I *do* need a rest. Would YOU like to sit on the egg in my nest?"
NARRATOR:	The elephant laughed.
HORTON:	"*Why of all silly things!* I haven't feathers and I haven't wings. ME on your egg? Why that doesn't make sense. . . . Your egg is so small, ma'am, and I'm so immense!"
MAYZIE:	"Tut, tut,"
NARRATOR:	answered Mayzie.
MAYZIE:	"I know you're not small But I'm *sure* you can do it. No trouble at all. Just sit on it softly. You're gentle and kind. Come, be a good fellow. I know you won't mind."
HORTON:	"I can't,"
NARRATOR:	said the elephant.
MAYZIE:	"PL-E-E-ASE!"
NARRATOR:	begged the bird.
MAYZIE:	"I won't be gone long, sir. I give you my word. I'll hurry right back. I'll never be missed. . . ."
HORTON:	"Very well,"
NARRATOR:	said the elephant,
HORTON:	"since you insist. . . . You want a vacation. Go fly off and take it. I'll sit on your egg and I'll try not to break it. I'll stay and be faithful. I mean what I say."

MAYZIE: "Toodle-oo!"
NARRATOR: sang out Mayzie and fluttered away.
HORTON: "H-m-m-m. . . the first thing to do is to prop up this tree
And make it much stronger. That *has* to be done
Before I get on it. I must weigh a ton."
NARRATOR: Then carefully,
Tenderly,
Gently he crept
Up the trunk to the nest where the little egg slept.
Then Horton the elephant smiled. Now that's that. . . .
And he sat
and he sat
and he sat. . . .
He sat all that day
And he kept that egg warm. . . .
And he sat all that night through a *terrible* storm.
It poured and it lightninged!
It thundered! It rumbled!
HORTON: "This isn't much fun,"
NARRATOR: The poor elephant grumbled.
HORTON: "I wish she'd come back
'Cause I'm cold and I'm wet.
I hope that that Mayzie bird doesn't forget."
NARRATOR: But Mayzie, by this time, was far beyond reach
Enjoying the sunshine way off in Palm Beach
And having *such* fun, such a wonderful rest,
Decided she'd NEVER go back to her nest! ! ! ![1]

UTILIZATION

17. Prepare a one to two minute speech in which you tell a ghost story, a suspense story, or a children's story. Demonstrate dynamic and animated vocal and physical behavior. Your speech will be evaluated against the criteria specified on the delivery evaluation form printed below.

Delivery Evaluation

Scale: 1–Weak; 2–Fair; 3–Average; 4–Good; and 5–Excellent.

		Comments
1. Stance & Movement	1 2 3 4 5	
2. Facial Expression	1 2 3 4 5	
3. Gestures	1 2 3 4 5	

4. Eye-Contact	1 2 3 4 5
5. Rate	1 2 3 4 5
6. Volume	1 2 3 4 5
7. Pitch	1 2 3 4 5
8. Quality	1 2 3 4 5
9. General Impression	1 2 3 4 5

Notes

1. From *Horton Hatches the Egg*, by Dr. Seuss and illustrated by Dr. Seuss. Copyright 1940 and renewed 1968 by Dr. Seuss. Reprinted by permission of Random House, Inc.

3

language

learning objectives

Recall
Comprehension
Application
Analysis
Synthesis

By the conclusion of this chapter you will be able to:

1. Name the three major qualities of effective language.

2. Match the three qualities of effective language with descriptions of those qualities.

3. Identify the quality of effective language violated by sample sentences.

4. Analyze speech fragments from the viewpoint of language qualities.

5. Construct passages that reflect the qualities of appropriateness, clarity, and vividness.

6. Name eight figures of speech.

7. Match eight definitions with the figures of speech they define.

8. Identify sample figures of speech by name.

9. Analyze the use of figures of speech in a sample speech.

10. Create fresh examples of at least six of the figures of speech.

11. Name the three strategies for arranging ideas through style.

12. Match the names of strategies for arranging ideas through style with descriptions of these strategies.

13. Identify speech fragments according to the stylistic strategy for arranging ideas employed.

14. Analyze the use of stylistic strategies for arranging ideas in a speech.

15. Construct a series of statements to illustrate each of the three stylistic strategies for arranging ideas.

Recall Comprehension Application Analysis Synthesis

16. Analyze the total use of language in a sample speech.

17. Construct a two-minute speech demonstrating effective use of language.

> Striking quality in speeches comes from the ability of the speaker to combine words in euphonious combinations, his ability to give poetic turns to wordings yet keep them prose, and his ability to paint word pictures which stir the listener's emotions.[1]
>
> Wilson and Arnold

Wilson and Arnold pay tribute to the power of language in making ideas striking and memorable. Careful attention to language, or the *style* of discourse, brings ideas alive and impresses them upon others. In this chapter we will begin by discussing the three qualities normally associated with an effective style. Consideration will then be given to common figures of speech and to stylistic strategies. Experience in using these devices and strategies will assist you in giving compelling expression to your ideas.

The Qualities of Effective Language

Since ancient times, most rhetorical theorists have agreed that the essential qualities that contribute to speaking excellence are *appropriateness, clarity,* and *vividness.*

Appropriateness

Language is *appropriate* when it is adapted to the speaker, the audience, and the occasion. Failure to adapt to any of these concerns may interfere with effective communication.

The *speaker's* use of language should seem natural to him or her. People who choose "impressive" words that are unfamiliar or use "big words" where they don't belong reveal to an audience that they are being less than genuine. Similarly, highly educated people who try to be "folksy" also do not ring true. We do not expect our neighbor to talk like the president of a university, nor do we expect a president of a university to talk like our neighbor.

Harry Truman provided an example of a speaker whose style appeared appropriate to his personality. His simple, direct style fit his origins as a Missouri farm boy and his practical approach to life. Consider Truman's use of language in a 1959 address to college students at Columbia University:

> I'm not impressed with this McCarthy idea of having students who have their education partly paid for by the government being forced

> to take a loyalty oath. They ought to learn what the government is about. But taking oaths won't teach them. Oaths are no substitute for teachers. I'll tell you something more about that tomorrow, because I think a test oath for students is silly (*applause*).[2]

His plain talk befitted the man and earned the audience's applause. However, such plain talk is not appropriate to all speakers. Howard Cosell has devoted a lifetime to acquiring and using elevated language and distinctive expressions to characterize everyday occurrences. Were Howard Cosell to engage in plain talk, he would seem both unnatural and insincere. Language is appropriate when it fits the character and experience of the speaker.

Language must also be appropriate to the background and interests of the *audience.* Stokely Carmichael provided an excellent illustration of this attribute in two speeches on black power. The following excerpt is from a speech addressed to a black audience in Detroit, Michigan.

> There's a thing called a syllogism. And it says like, if you're born in Detroit, you're beautiful; that's the major premise. The minor premise is—I am born in Detroit. Therefore, I am beautiful. Anything all black is bad—major premise. Minor premise—I am all black. Therefore [pause], yeah, yeah [laughter and applause] yeah. You're all out there, and the man telling you that anything all black is bad, and you talking about yourself, and you don't even know it. You ain't never heard no white people say that anything all white is bad. You ain't never heard them say it. They only starting to get upset now because we're going for some power. Before they didn't never criticize the fact that their government was all white and was nothing but power, that's white power [applause]. They didn't say nothing about that [continued applause].[3]

The second example is from Carmichael's address on black power to a white audience at Wisconsin State University, Whitewater, Wisconsin.

> One of the most pointed illustrations of the need for Black Power, as a positive and redemptive force in a society degenerating into a form of totalitarianism, is to be made by examining the history of distortion that the concept has received in national media of publicity. In this "debate," as in everything else that affects our lives, Blacks are dependent on, and at the discretion of, forces and institutions within the white society which have little interest in representing us honestly. Our experience with the national press has been that where they have managed to escape a meretricious special interest in "Git Whitey" sensationalism and race-war mongering, individual reporters and commentators have been conditioned by the enveloping racism of the society to the point where they are incapable even of objective ob-

> servation and reporting of racial *incidents,* much less the analysis of *ideas.* But this limitation of vision and perceptions is an inevitable consequence of the dictatorship of definition, interpretation and consciousness, along with the censorship of history that the society has inflicted upon the Black—and itself.[4]

The difference in style is remarkable, isn't it? Carmichael adapted to the black audience by using a colloquial style; his expressions were in the idiom of the audience he addressed. When he appeared before a white audience in a college environment, Carmichael abandoned the casual, informal style in favor of a studied, intellectual style. As this example demonstrates, the audience addressed should strongly influence the language choices a speaker makes.

The adaptation of language to *occasion* is the third attribute of appropriateness. The style should match the formality of the occasion. To demonstrate how the requirements of occasion influence a speaker's choices, consider the following two examples. Ross Smyth, speaking to Rotary Club members on the subject of humor in public speaking, adopted an easy, colloquial style:

> Any person who has to give a speech . . . should insert a little humour or levity into it. "Now, wait a minute," you'll say to me, "I can't match Bob Hope, Wayne and Shuster or Rich Little—so what's the use of trying." You don't have to compete with these full-time professional humorists. Let's look at it this way. . . .[5]

Contrast this with the following excerpt from a speech delivered on nationwide television by Gerald Ford:

> On the higher plane of public morality, there is no need for me to preach tonight. We have thousands of far better preachers and millions of sacred scriptures to guide us on the path of personal right-living and exemplary official conduct.[6]

While the easy familiarity of Mr. Smyth was appropriate for an after-dinner speech, it would not fit the situation facing Gerald Ford as he addressed the American public and the world shortly after assuming office.

Clarity

If the audience does not understand your message, it may be that your ideas lack *clarity,* the second major quality of effective language. The achievement of clarity is dependent on the use of *simple, specific* expressions.

Simplicity of style means substituting little words for big ones. Instead of saying "the chemical has an oxygenous quality," isn't it clearer to say "the chemical is gaslike?" Instead of saying "the argument produced a dialectical tension, which threatened to destroy the symbiotic relationship," isn't just as much information communicated by saying "the argument created tension, which threatened to destroy the marriage?" The addition of "dialectical" and "symbiotic" may be construed as display language rather than as a serious attempt to communicate.

Simple words must, however, be arranged in proper order to ensure that meaning is conveyed. In discussing problems encountered in understanding messages, Gerald Goldhaber related the following examples, drawn from letters on file at a Veterans Administration office:

> Both sides of my parents are poor and I can't expect nothing from them, as my mother has been in bed for one year with the same doctor, and won't change.
>
> I am forwarding you my marriage certificate and my 2 children, one is a mistake as you can plainly see.
>
> In accordance with your instructions, I have given birth to twins in the enclosed envelope.[7]

In what must qualify as an understatement, Goldhaber observed that "the senders of the above letters may not have had the same meanings in their minds as may be interpreted by some readers." In Goldhaber's examples, ambiguous phrasing, not the choice of big words, was responsible for a lack of clarity. A simple style does not mean that your expression must be pedestrian. John Paul Jones' "I have not yet begun to fight," and Paul Revere's "the Redcoats are coming" are simple, yet forceful expressions. The use of simple words, properly arranged within sentences may produce striking, uncommon expressions. In view of the increasing use of big words where little ones will do, an audience may be thankful if they can simply understand you.

The second attribute of clarity is *specificity*. Vague and ambiguous language may conceal the speaker's meaning. As an example of ambiguous language, consider the following quotation from a college commencement speech on student attitudes toward life-style:

> This attitude is reasonable for there are only a handful of dialectics whose polarities compete for the loyalty of the social community. Each holds the stage for about a century before yielding to its counterpart who demands equal opportunity to direct man's life. One of these guiding ideas pivots on a distinction between form and content; the

> style of a message in contrast to its meaning, or speaking more euphemistically, music in contradistinction to words. When we live under the unquestioned reign of one, the other rests in shadows, and ordinarily we do not regard it as a serious possibility for directing a life. But when it creeps out of the darkness and challenges the persuasive power of its rival, parading its intuitive attractiveness, we become acutely aware of the choice each of us had but did not recognize.[8]

Besides violating the attribute of simplicity (one may wonder what "a handful of dialectics whose polarities compete" means), the passage violates the attribute of specificity by presenting vague generalities rather than concrete illustrations. In contrast to this example of nonspecific language, consider the impact of specific language on a student's description of a special place where friends gathered to sort out their "mangled minds":

> And so they came to Hickory in summer and winter, in rain or snow, by car or snowmobile, singly, in pairs, in carloads, from miles around, from many schools, from many ways of life, and they sat around a blazing fire in the midst of a clearing hemmed by tall pines and played, and talked, and laughed, and sang, and were themselves. A spirit of camaraderie, and youth and strength pervaded. Crazy things were done, and still crazier things said. They laughed; they smoked; they drank; they made love; and they grew by it and learned from it that they were people too.[9]

The passage creates a clear picture of Hickory through its attention to specific details. In addition, the speaker may have succeeded in reminding audience members of similar experiences in their pasts. Simple and specific language will enable you to give clear expression to your ideas.

Vividness

Vividness is that quality of style that renders ideas compelling and memorable. The primary attributes of a vivid style are *forcefulness* and *freshness*.

A *forceful* style rivets the attention of an audience on the speaker's subject. Senator George Vest provided an excellent example of a forceful style. Called on to assist in a trial involving a suit over the death of a dog, Senator Vest pleaded for damages in these words:

> Gentlemen of the Jury—The best friend a man has in the world may turn against him and become his enemy. The son or daughter that he has reared with loving care may prove ungrateful. Those who are

> nearest and dearest to us, those whom we trust with our happiness and our good name may become traitors to their faith. The money that a man has he may lose. It flies away from him, perhaps, when he needs it most. A man's reputation may be sacrificed in a moment of ill-considered action. The people who are prone to fall on their knees to do us honor when success is with us may be the first to throw the stone of malice when failure settles its cloud on our heads. The one absolutely unselfish friend that man can have in this selfish world, the one that never proves ungrateful or treacherous, is his dog. A man's dog stands by him in prosperity and poverty, in health and sickness. He will sleep on the cold ground, where the wintry winds blow, and the snow drives fiercely, if only he may be near his master's side. He will kiss the hand that has no food to offer; he will lick the wounds and sores that come in encounter with the roughness of the world. He guards the sleep of his pauper master as if he were a prince. When all other friends desert, he remains. When riches take wings and reputation falls to pieces, he is as constant in his love as the sun in its journeys through the heavens. If fortune drives the master forth an outcast in the world, friendless and homeless, the faithful dog asks no higher privilege than that of accompanying him, to guard against danger, to fight against his enemies. And when the last scene of all comes, and death takes the master in his embrace, and his body is laid away in the cold ground, no matter if all other friends pursue their way, there, by the graveside, will the noble dog be found, his head between his paws, his eyes sad, but open to alert watchfulness, faithful and true, even to death.[10]

The powerfulness of the message touched the hearts of both judge and jury; at the end they were in tears. Although he ignored the legal "facts" of the case, Senator Vest succeeded in obtaining damages for his client: the jury awarded damages of $500, $300 more than had been asked for by the plaintiff!

In judging the forceful, compelling nature of language, you might ask yourself how often an audience's attention would have strayed if Lincoln had spoken these words at Gettysburg:

> I haven't checked these figures but eighty-seven years ago, I think it was, a number of individuals organized a governmental setup here in this country, I believe it covered certain eastern areas, with this idea they were following up based on a sort of national-independence arrangement and the program that every individual is just as good as every other individual. Well, now,of course we are dealing with this big difference of opinion, civil disturbance you might say, although I don't like to appear to take sides or name any individuals, and the point is naturally to check up, by actual experience in the field, to see whether any government setup with a basis like the one I was mentioning has

any validity, whether that dedication, you might say, by those early individuals will pay off in lasting values.

Well, here we are, you might put it that way, all together at the scene where one of these disturbances between different sides got going. We want to pay our tribute to those loved ones, those departed individuals who made the supreme sacrifice here on the basis of their opinions about how this setup ought to be handled. It is absolutely in order and one hundred percent okay to do this.

But if you look at the over-all picture of this, we can't pay any tribute—we can't sanctify this area—we can't hallow according to whatever individuals' creeds or faiths or sort of religious outlooks are involved—like I said about this very particular area. It was those individuals themselves, including the enlisted men, very brave individuals, who have given this religious character to the area. The way I see it, the rest of the world will not remember any statements issued here but it will never forget how these men put their shoulders to the wheel and carried this idea down the fairway.

Our job, the living individuals' job here, is to pick up the burden and sink the putt they made these big efforts here for. It is our job to get on with the assignment—and from these deceased fine individuals to take extra inspiration, you could call it, for the same theories about which they did such a lot.

We have to make up our minds right here and now, as I see it, that they didn't put out all that blood, perspiration and—well—that they didn't just make a dry run here, and that all of us here, under God, that is, the God of our choice, shall beef up this idea about freedom and liberty and those kind of arrangements, and that government of all individuals, by all individuals, and for the individuals, shall not pass out of the world-picture.[11]

Deliberately composed by Oliver Jensen, editor of *American Heritage,* the above passage does not succeed in arousing an audience's attention through forceful language. This example also violates the second attribute of a vivid style—*freshness.*

The contrast between Jensen's paraphrase and Lincoln's original statement is striking:

I haven't checked these figures, but eighty-seven years ago	Four score and seven years ago . . . .
. . . the program that every individual is just as good as every other individual.	. . . the proposition that all men are created equal.
. . . that government of all individuals, by all individuals, and for the individuals, shall not pass out of the world-picture.	. . . that government of the people, by the people, and for the the people shall not perish from this earth.[12]

The language of Jensen is stale and ordinary; the language of Lincoln is fresh and distinctive. Another example of freshness may be found in a eulogy to Winston S. Churchill, in which Adlai Stevenson expressed his sense of loss in these words:

> We shall hear no longer the remembered eloquence and wit, the old courage and defiance, the robust serenity of indomitable faith. Our world is thus poorer, our political dialogue is diminished and the sources of public inspiration run more thinly for all of us. There is a lonesome place against the sky.[13]

The metaphorical allusion to a "lonesome place against the sky" is both striking and fresh. It portrays the world's loss with greater intensity than "We are sorry he's gone," or "It is sad that he has died."

As you create a brisk, lively style, avoid expressions that are well-known and over-used. Consider the lack of freshness in the following examples:

> Let us not wallow in the valley of despair.[14]
>
> There is plenty of rough road up ahead.[15]
>
> [These questions] served to keep us on our toes.[16]
>
> We've recognized the dangers . . . of wearing a well-beaten path to the short-term money market.[17]

The last example illustrates a misuse of images: "wearing" conflicts with the image of a pathway which is already "well-beaten." "Trodding" might be a better choice. Freshness may turn to foolishness when you mix metaphors:

> What we have to do is take the bull by the tail and look the situation in the face.—Minnesota Congressman Magnus Johnson.
>
> When I smell a rat, I nip it in the bud.—An unidentified politician, March 3, 1961.[18]

Unless you intend to make some novel use of a "dead" expression, such as "War is hell," you will be better off creating original phrases that will add both freshness and vitality to your discourse.

EXERCISES

VERIFICATION

1. Identify the qualities of effective language discussed in the text.

   a.

b.

c.

VERIFICATION

2. Match the three qualities of effective language with the descriptions provided below.

   a. ____________________ The style is forceful and memorable.

   b. ____________________ The style is adapted to the audience, occasion, subject, and speaker.

   c. ____________________ The style is both simple and specific.

UTILIZATION

3. Identify the quality of effective language violated in each of the following examples.

   a. ____________________ He is inebriated by the exuberance of his own verbosity.

   b. ____________________ The old man was hard as a rock, and his face was wrinkled like a prune.

   c. ____________________ As I look back to the four years preceding this, my inauguration, all I can say is "That's a hell of a way to run a country."

UTILIZATION

4. Analyze the following speech fragment from the perspective of the qualities of effective language.

   (Jenkin Lloyd Jones, Editor and Publisher of the *Tulsa Tribune,* spoke before the Ohio Chamber of Commerce on the topic "Let's Bring Back Dad.")

> I would submit, ladies and gentlemen, that the children of the so-called class which we represent is the worst-raised generation in the history of America. And who raised them? We did! Who tried to buy their love with material things for which they were not ready? We did. Who sought to gain status by seeing to it that our kid was the first kid on the block with a new gizmo? We did.
>
> What generation produced a federal judiciary that has so fuzzed up the common sense definition of dirt that our youngsters are drowned in porno? Our generation. Who produced the Hollywood that's willing to do anything for a buck and comes out with movies that would better be described as peep-shows or as visual aids in an abnormal psych class and that lards and meringues and whipped creams its hypocrisy by claiming that it is struggling toward new horizons in intellectual freedom? That's our generation. We sit behind the box office; we give

the youngsters two bucks or two and a half to go out and see GP rated up from R and R rated up from X. I remember in my generation we were lucky to get a dime to go out and see Tom Mix and Hoot Gibson kiss their horses.

Who raised the most lopsided generation in human history? We did. Who collapsed when little Phyllis went into a tantrum because Mary's mother was going to let her go steady at thirteen? And who hurled little Phyllis into a premature monogamy for which she was not physically or psychologically prepared? And who is reaping the whirlwind? We are.[19]

UTILIZATION

5. Working in triads, complete the following three exercises on a separate sheet of paper.
   a. Rewrite the following paragraph to make it *appropriate* not only to the immediate audience but also to the larger national audience.

      A political candidate delivers a speech on housing at a local meeting of the Italian Citizen's League: "Ladies and Gentlemen, I take pleasure in the opportunity to meet with you and discuss the great issues of the day. As regards the subject of housing, you may rest assured that I shall forever fight to maintain the ethnic purity of every neighborhood, whether black, white, red, or yellow."
   b. Rewrite the following paragraph so that the speaker's ideas emerge with *clarity*.

      "Whenever people complain about taxation, they generally fail to realize that the taxes they pay buy services. A rational approach to the problem of taxation requires that individuals candidly assess their own values, their own needs, and their own views of the importance of the services that are offered. Only through such value-oriented, retrospective reflections can we gain true insight into the pervasive, timeless problems generated by the interface of the consumption ethic with fiscal and economic accountability."
   c. List three to five synonyms for each of the following word clusters: "little town," "sunset," "gloom," and "settled upon." Drawing from your list of synonyms, rewrite the following sentence in a *vivid* way: "At sunset, gloom settled on the little town."

Choosing Stylistic Devices

An energetic style may be achieved by careful choice of figurative language. Generally called "figures of speech," the following eight stylistic devices are useful in giving compelling expression to your ideas.

Simile

A simile directly compares two essentially dissimilar objects. It is characterized by the use of "like" or "as" in connecting ideas that are figuratively compared. The expression "Like a raging tornado, the mob tore through the town destroying everything in its path" is an example of a simile. Marie Ransley used the following simile in explaining the role of marshes in absorbing agricultural run-off: "Keeping the marshes which surround the lakes would alleviate some of this problem, since *marshes work like sponges* in soaking up nutrients." [20] The primary function of a simile is to offer a concrete, familiar "interpretation" of an abstract or unfamiliar concept. An undergraduate student illustrated the use of a simile in describing the Phillipine Islands: "They lie like broken pieces of emerald that were dropped into the South China Sea by some giant." [21] When your object is to explain an idea or describe a place in clear, familiar, forceful language, a simile may be a useful tool.

Metaphor

A metaphor asserts an implied comparison between dissimilar objects or ideas. It is distinguished from a simile by the omission of "like" or "as" in asserting the comparison. The expressions "He is a snake" and "America is a rudderless ship adrift in the sea of world politics" are examples of metaphors. As in the case of similes, metaphors are useful devices for explaining the abstract or unknown in more concrete language, or for presenting striking contrasts in vivid terms. For example, Martin Luther King, Jr. expressed the plight of the Negro: "The Negro lives on a lonely island of poverty in the midst of a vast ocean of material prosperity." [22] Similarly, John F. Kennedy expressed the indispensible role of "intellectuals" through this metaphor: "the political profession needs to have its temperature lowered in the cooling waters of the scholastic pool." [23] In both cases, the expressions are more powerful than if the speakers had said "The Negro is alone in his poverty," or "The politician can learn from the intellectual."

In the preceding examples, metaphors were contained in single sentences. However, metaphors also may be used in highlighting a theme or idea for an entire speech. Ina Brownlee Bragdon exemplified this usage in a speech on migrant children.[24] In order to convey the lives of these children in forceful, vivid terms, Ms. Bragdon adopted the metaphor of a "mask." Used in its normal setting, a mask is a physical object that covers a person's face. In her speech, Ms. Bragdon spoke of the circumstances that "have forced the disadvantaged children to wear certain 'masks' which cause many misunderstandings and misconceptions." She highlighted several: "the mask of periodic 'tuning-out,'" "the mask of blank stares," and "the mask of ignorance." Finally, she asked questions such as "Why bother to lift the masks?" and "What will be found underneath the masks?" In this manner, "masks" became a controlling metaphor for the entire speech and lent it more force and vitality than would be present if the speaker merely said "some children tune-out, look blank, and seem ignorant." Whether used in single sentences or as a controlling expression for a speech, metaphors are valuable for achieving an appropriate, clear, and vivid style.

Personification

A speaker employs personification when he or she endows inanimate objects or animals with human traits or attributes. Examples of personification include expressions such as:

> The old roof groaned in pain under the weight of the new fallen snow.
>
> America's courage is to be found in the resoluteness of her citizenry.
>
> The little train, exhausted from its long, arduous climb, paused for breath before beginning the descent into the valley below.

Gerald Krause sharpened an image of a Philippine scene through the use of this device:

> Coconut palms hold up the sky, while lazy clouds watch naked children playing tag with the waves. Fishing boats, painted in psychedelic pinks, greens, and oranges split the waves and make the sea give up her harvest.[25]

Martin Luther King, Jr. imparted human qualities to truth:

> We shall overcome because there is something in this universe that justifies William Cullen Bryant in saying that truth crushed to earth shall rise again. . . . there is something in this universe that justifies James Russell Lowell in saying, truth forever on the scaffold, wrong forever on the throne.[26]

Whether your nonhuman subject is an island scene or truth, you can lend a sense of power and beauty to your discussion by using personification.

Hyperbole

This device exaggerates the actual situation being represented. You may have used an expression similar to the following hyperboles:

Even a sparrow is smarter than you.

I'm so hungry I could eat my arm.

It's so hot you could fry an egg on the sidewalk.

Doubtless, you can think of many other expressions which are exaggerations of the actual state of your intelligence, hunger, or feelings about the heat. These and other topics discussed in casual, informal settings are frequently expressed as hyperboles for dramatic effect. In more formal settings, a speaker may exaggerate the choices faced by his or her audience in order to inspire them to action. Dr. Jerome Kagen, a Professor of Human Development at Harvard University, introduced his subject with this statement:

> We face two great crises on your commencement day—a frightening division between rich and poor Americans that tears at the increasingly frail cohesiveness of our community, and a dissolution of the basic values that have guided the direction of many lives for many centuries.[27]

The situation may not be this drastic, but the exaggeration may be a justifiable means of arousing an audience's interest in the subject. In a similar fashion Robert V. Andelson used hyperbole to express his disgust with the liberal reaction to activism:

> Too many of our educational administrators . . . seem to be saying, "Right on! Do your thing! And if your thing happens to be arson, who am I to criticize? In fact, if you'll permit me, I'll hand you the matches just to show how liberal I am." [28]

While it is doubtful that any administrator *would* say this, Andelson created a stronger, more forceful expression of his feeling than if he had said, "Some administrators are permissive." When faced with the need to inspire your audience, overcome apathy, or simply phrase a situation in dramatic terms, hyperbole may be an effective stylistic device.

Understatement

Understatement, the opposite of hyperbole, involves a conservative expression of an actual state of affairs. Introducing Mark Spitz, winner of seven Olympic gold medals, by saying "He is a pretty good swimmer" understates his ability. Likewise, to summarize the coaching career of John Wooden, former coach of the UCLA Bruins, by saying "he was a pretty fair coach; he won most of his games" is a severe understatement of Wooden's accomplishments. Were one to say "it's wet outside" in the face of a lengthy monsoon, one would be using understatement to place the actual state of affairs in sharp relief. Like hyperbole, understatement may be used to dramatize the situation being discussed. The disparity between the expression and the reality it represents focuses audience attention on the subject in a powerful and vivid manner. It is likely that William Pinson's audience at a seminar sponsored by the Southern Baptist Convention regarded the following expressions as understatements: "*Playboy* talks about sex more than any other subject;" "The view of modern life presented by *Playboy* is less than realistic." [29] To a Baptist audience, *Playboy* is preoccupied with sex and represents a grossly distorted view of life. As this example suggests, understatement depends to a great extent on the audience's perception of reality.

Irony

Irony uses specific words or phrases to depict a situation that appears to be the opposite of what should be the case. Irony often occurs in everyday conversations: "With friends like you, who needs enemies." Irony may also be found in public utterances. When Adlai Stevenson lost the 1956 presidential election, he recalled Abraham Lincoln's statement: "It hurts too much to laugh, but I'm too old to cry." Felipe V. Ponce, Jr. employed irony in his characterization of the history of his people:

> The history of today's Chicano dates back to the time of the Aztecs and other sixteenth-century Indian tribes. They were noble lords of a culture that was one of the high points of civilization. Along came the Spaniards, Christians who looted, murdered, and raped, and for their crimes were promptly knighted.[30]

Where one would expect punishment to be given, the Spaniards and Christians were rewarded. Irony is a powerful means of illustrating injustices or conveying a satiric picture of events.

Alliteration

Whenever a speaker uses the same sound to begin a series of words, the style is alliterative. Adlai Stevenson illustrated the use of alliteration in this example: "Repetition, reiteration, rhetoric have all rubbed off the cutting edge.[31] In more recent times, Spiro Agnew's "nattering nabobs of negativism"[32] stands out as a dramatic use of alliteration to describe the actions of activists opposed to the United States' involvement in Vietnam. Alliteration conveys a sense of rhythm and vitality lacking in an expression similar in meaning. How much more vivid and memorable is "nattering nabobs of negativism" than is "vocal critics of governmental policy."

Imagery

A metaphor creates a *new* relationship between ideas or events; imagery recreates a scene.[33] When executed well, imagery brings a scene before the audience with such clarity as to make them "see" the events depicted. In creating a "you are there" feeling, imagery may employ some of the stylistic devices already covered in this discussion. In his "Farewell to the Cadets," General Douglas MacArthur painted this portrait of the American soldier:

> From one end of the world to the other, he has drained deep the chalice of courage. As I listened to those songs, in memory's eye I could see those staggering columns of the First World War, bending under soggy packs on many a weary march, from dripping dusk to drizzling dawn, slogging ankle-deep through the mire of shell-shocked roads; to form grimly for the attack, blue-lipped, covered with sludge and mud, chilled by the wind and rain, driving home to their objective, and, for many, to the judgment seat of God.[34]

Elizabeth Langer provided a striking example of imagery in her eulogy to the incomparable orchestra conductor, Arturo Toscanini:

> Arturo Toscanini led his farewell concert on April 4, 1954. Carnegie Hall overflowed with his admirers and his life-long friends. As the lights began to dim, a dignified man walked slowly to his earned position at the center of the stage. He was short of stature; but walked with a confidence reminiscent of a once bursting energy. His long-flowing white hair, deep-set moist eyes, expressive thin fingers, suggested the lovable quality of the true artist. His manner was serene and unpretentious. Throughout the performance of Wagner, one of the Maestro's favorite composers, a loving audience wept shamelessly as it watched the quality of the Maestro's work deteriorate before its eyes. His strength was gone, and he had no heart for his music. A few times he gripped a nearby rail for support. And the concert ended with Toscanini only beating time. He had once said to his close friends, probably those in the audience at that very moment, "When the baton

> trembles in my hand, I shall conduct no more." The baton did tremble that night, and Arturo Toscanini never conducted again. And on January 17 of this year, the great Maestro died at fourscore and nine.[35]

With attention to detail, an image can become a powerful means of arousing an audience's feelings and intensifying their involvement in your speech.

EXERCISES

VERIFICATION

6. Identify the eight figures of speech.

VERIFICATION

7. Match the figures of speech in question 6 with the descriptions that follow. (Caution: Two of the descriptions do not apply.)

   a. ______________ Words in sequence begin with the same sound.

   b. ______________ The speaker attributes human qualities to nonhuman things.

   c. ______________ The speaker employs a direct comparison between two dissimilar things.

   d. ______________ The speaker's language recreates a scene.

   e. ______________ The figure substitutes a part for a whole.

   f. ______________ The characterization of reality is conservatively stated.

   g. ______________ The comparison between dissimilar things is implied.

   h. ______________ A speaker uses a word in a manner opposite to the word's normal meaning.

i. ______________________ The characterization of an event or feeling is exaggerated.

j. ______________________ A series of sentences begin with the same phrase.

UTILIZATION

8. Identify by name each of the sample figures of speech presented below. If the sample does not match any of the devices discussed, leave the space blank.

a. ______________________ I was so scared when I got up to speak, I thought I would die.

b. ______________________ The heavy demolition ball lunged forward, eagerly attacking the dilapidated building.

c. ______________________ Apathy is a disease of the soul.

d. ______________________ Gone are the values we cherish. Gone is the courage to fight against a foe. Gone is the strength to withstand adversity. Gone is our sense of pride in our accomplishments.

e. ______________________ Creative, constructive, concerned—these are the characteristics of our generation.

f. ______________________ I'm so happy about your spending our last dollar on a chance in the Irish Sweepstakes.

g. ______________________ The farmer surveyed his devastated cornfield then remarked dryly, "Looks like we had a little hail last night."

h. ______________________ As the twig is bent, so grows the tree. A child, like the twig, grows as he is shaped during his youth.

i. ______________________ Where the tall oak stood, a concrete column now stands. Where green grass grew in the shade of the oak, pigeons now pick away at nonexistent crumbs on a gleaming marble surface. Where young couples sat gaily in the comfort of that old oak, none now linger. All this in the name of progress.

UTILIZATION

9. Analyze the use of figurative language in the sample presented below.

In a sense we have come to our nation's capitol to cash a check. When the architects of our republic wrote the magnificent words of the Constitution and the Declaration of Independence, they were signing a promissory note to which every American was to fall heir. This note was a promise that all men, yes, black men as well as white men, would be guaranteed the unalienable rights of life, liberty, and the pursuit of happiness.

It is obvious today that America has defaulted on this promissory note insofar as her citizens of color are concerned. Instead of honoring this sacred obligation, America has given the Negro people a bad check, which has come back marked "insufficient funds."

But we refuse to believe that the bank of justice is bankrupt. We refuse to believe that there are insufficient funds in the great vaults of opportunity of this nation.[36]

UTILIZATION

10. A stimulus phrase or a description of the task is provided for each figure of speech. Create a fresh example of at least six of the eight figures.

Personification: Using the stimulus sentence as a guide, create a personification of your home town.

"Gary, Indiana awakens with grimy face and coughs its greeting to the new day."

Simile: Good food is like ____________________.

Understatement: Mohammed Ali is ____________________.

Alliteration: D____________________, d____________________, and d____________________ are what this country is all about.

Metaphor: Adolescence is ____________________.

Hyperbole: I'm so hungry I could ____________________.

Irony: It was a really neat dance, considering ____________________.

Imagery: Recreate the image of a jogger in vivid language:

Choosing Stylistic Strategies

Very often, a speaker's ideas may lend themselves to stylistic applications that are more extensive than the figures of speech we have considered. Style may be used to order ideas within a paragraph and may enhance idea development between and among paragraphs within a speech. In this section we will consider three strategies for structuring ideas through style: climax, antithesis, and parallelism.

Climax

This strategy arranges ideas in an ascending order, with the final idea being the most powerful in the series. Consider Adlai Stevenson's closing comments in his eulogy to Winston Churchill:

> The great aristocrat, the beloved leader, the profound historian, the gifted painter, the superb politician, the lord of language, the orator, the wit—yes, and the dedicated bricklayer—behind all of them was the man of simple faith, steadfast in defeat, generous in victory, resigned in age, trusting in a loving providence and committing his achievements and his triumphs to a higher power.
>
> Like the patriarchs of old, he waited on God's judgment and it could be said of him—as of the immortals that went before him—that God "magnified him in the fear of his enemies and with his words he made prodigies to cease. He glorified him in the sight of kings and gave him commandments in the sight of his people. He showed him his Glory and sanctified him in his faith . . . ."[37]

From specifics to God's judgment, the ending is a fitting climax to an eloquent tribute to one of our century's leading statesmen. In an appeal for understanding, Felipe Ponce, Jr. brought his audience from a consideration of specific features to a general appraisal of the La Causa movement:

> The Chicano Movement is here. "La Raza" or "Our People" are organizing and petitioning for their rights. The nine million people who became citizens of this country willingly or unwillingly are no longer willing to accept the inequities in education, employment, and housing which have been part of our lives. We are reevaluating our culture and realizing that it is a thing to be preserved, indeed treasured. In short, we are coming to grips with our reality and a strong sense of unity is developing across the nation. La Causa is growing in momentum and its people, the Chicanos, are growing in pride, dignity, and determination.[38]

Although these examples are from conclusions to speeches, a climatic ordering may occur at any point in a speech. The movement of ideas may be given greater strength and impact when arranged through attention to this strategy.

Antithesis

Antithesis strikes a balance between opposites within a single sentence. It depends both on successful word choice and the proper placement of words within a sentence. John F. Kennedy's famous line "Ask not what your country can do for you—ask what you can do for your country" is a classic example of an antithetical expression. The ideas are of equal strength and are opposed to one another. The following excerpt from a speech by Sydney Smith illustrates the use of antithesis in structuring ideas within paragraphs:

> You have freedom of choice, and by inescapable equations your choices will bring you profit or loss. If you choose to work, you will pass; if you don't, you will fail. If you neglect your work, you will dislike it; if you do it well, you will enjoy it. If you join little cliques, you will be self-satisfied; if you make friends widely, you will be interesting. If you act like a boor, you will be despised; if you act like a human being, you will be respected. If you spurn wisdom, wise people will spurn you; if you seek wisdom, they will seek you. If you adopt a pose of boredom, you will be a bore; if you show vitality, you will be alive. If you spend your free time playing bridge, you will be a good bridge player; if you spend it reading, discussing and thinking of things that matter, you will be an educated person.[39]

As this example illustrates, antithesis compresses opposing notions into clear alternatives. The forcefulness of the device is apparent in Pinson's summary of Hugh Hefner's *Playboy* philosophy: "What Hefner's argument really says is that we ought to make our creed match our deeds instead of making our deeds match our creed." [40] Whether used as a single expression within a paragraph, or in an extended series, antithesis provides a sense of rhythm and balance within your speech.

Parallelism

Parallelism gives equal ideas equal status. A well-known example is Lincoln's "government of the people, by the people, and for the people." Parallelism establishes a rhythmic quality in the discourse. Another well-known example is found in Martin Luther King's speech, "I Have a Dream":

> And so let freedom ring from the prodigious hilltops of New Hampshire.
> Let freedom ring from the mighty mountains of New York.
> Let freedom ring from the heightening Alleghenies of Pennsylvania.
> Let freedom ring from the snow-capped Rockies of Colorado.
> Let freedom ring from the curvaceous slopes of California.
> But not only that.
> Let freedom ring from Stone Mountain of Georgia.
> Let freedom ring from Lookout Mountain of Tennessee.

> Let freedom ring from every hill and molehill of Mississippi, from every mountainside, let freedom ring.[41]

The following example also displays an effective use of parallelism in conveying an idea:

> Too many of our educational administrators seem to feel the way Professor Mallard does. Too many of them seem to be saying, "Right on! Do your thing!" . . . Too many of them seem to think that creative dialogue is possible with barbarians whose vocabulary consists mainly of four-letter words. Too many of them seem to believe that campuses should be privileged sanctuaries for those who openly express contempt for law and order. Too many of them seem to have the notion that it is somehow ungentlemanly to deal firmly and decisively with disruption.[42]

Although you may disagree with Professor Andelson's sentiments, there is no mistaking the sentiments themselves. Through an apt use of parallel style, he has conveyed his attitude toward weak-kneed academics in succinct, lucid phrases.

Whether you use climax, antithesis, or parallel structure, the elegance and crispness of your speech can be immeasurably strengthened through such strategies.

EXERCISES

VERIFICATION

11. Identify the three strategies for arranging ideas through style.

    a.

    b.

    c.

VERIFICATION

12. Using the answers from 11 above, match the three strategies for arranging ideas through style with the descriptions provided below. (Caution: There is one distractor.)

    a. ____________________ presents opposite ideas in balanced order.

    b. ____________________ arrangement which builds in emotional impact.

    c. ____________________ begins a series of words with the same sounds.

    d. ____________________ constructs similar ideas in similar form.

UTILIZATION

13. Identify the stylistic strategy for arranging ideas in the following passages.

a. ____________________ The conservative looks to the past; the liberal looks to the present.
The conservative looks to what was, the liberal looks to what should be.
The conservative looks to what tradition demands, the liberal looks to what humanity demands.

b. ____________________ Edward Kennedy has been a leader in Congress.
Edward Kennedy has been a steady advocate of liberal reforms.
Edward Kennedy has been a watchdog over the abuse of federal power.
Edward Kennedy has been a potent ally of social equality and civil rights.

c. ____________________ The shadows are lengthening for me. The twilight is here. My days of old have vanished—tone and tints. They have gone glimmering through the dreams of things that were. Their memory is one of wondrous beauty watered by tears and coaxed and caressed by the smiles of yesterday. I listen vainly, but with thirsty ear, for the witching melody of faint bugles blowing reveille, of far drums beating the long roll.

In my dreams I hear again the crash of guns, the rattle of musketry, the strange, mournful mutter of the battlefield. But in the evening of my memory always I come back to West Point. Always there echoes and re-echoes: duty, honor, country.

Today marks my final roll call with you. But I want you to know that when I cross the river, my last conscious thoughts will be of the Corps, and the Corps, and the Corps.

I bid you farewell.[43]

UTILIZATION

14. Analyze the following speech fragment from the perspective of stylistic strategies for arranging ideas.

So I say to you, my friends, that even though we must face the difficulties of today and tomorrow, I still have a dream. It is a dream deeply rooted in the American dream that one day this nation will rise up and live out the true meaning of its creed—we hold these truths to be self-evident, that all men are created equal.

I have a dream that one day on the red hills of Georgia, sons of former slaves and sons of former slaveowners will be able to sit down together at the table of brotherhood.

I have a dream that one day, even the state of Mississippi, a state sweltering with the heat of injustice, sweltering with the heat of oppression, will be transformed into an oasis of freedom and justice.

I have a dream my four little children will one day live in a nation where they will not be judged by the color of their skin but by content of their character. I have a dream today!

I have a dream that one day, down in Alabama, with its vicious racists, with its governor having his lips dripping with the words of interposition and nullification, that one day, right there in Alabama, little black boys and black girls will be able to join hands with little white boys and white girls as sisters and brothers. I have a dream today!

I have a dream that one day every valley shall be exalted, every hill and mountain shall be made low, the rough places shall be made plain, and the crooked places shall be made straight and the glory of the Lord will be revealed and all flesh shall see it together.

This is our hope. This is the faith that I go back to the South with.

With this faith we will be able to hew out of the mountain of despair a stone of hope. With this faith we will be able to transform the jangling discords of our nation into a beautiful symphony of brotherhood.[44]

UTILIZATION

15. Complete the following activities on a separate sheet of paper.
    a. Construct a series of five antithetical statements that contrasts two people, places, things, concepts, etc. (liberal/conservative). By the end of your antithesis it should be clear which of the pair you favor.
    b. Construct a series of four or five statements on the same subject such that each surpasses the preceding in terms of emotional impact.
    c. Construct a series of three to five statements on the same subject using parallelism in structure.

Putting It All Together

In this chapter we have attempted to stimulate your interest in effective language usage. As you create your own speeches, keep in mind the qualities of style, the various figures of speech, and the stylistic strategies that may be employed to enhance the power of your ideas. The following outline may be helpful.

Style Checklist

1. Does your speech contain these qualities and attributes?
   a. Appropriateness—Speaker
Audience
Occasion
   b. Clarity— Simplicity
Specificity
   c. Vividness— Forcefulness
Freshness
2. Can your subject be enlivened by one or more of these figures of speech?
   a. Simile
   b. Metaphor
   c. Personification
   d. Hyperbole
   e. Understatement
   f. Irony
   g. Alliteration
   h. Imagery
3. Can your ideas be arranged through the use of one of these strategies?
   a. Climax
   b. Antithesis
   c. Parallelism

A Speech That Demonstrates Variety in Style

President John F. Kennedy's inaugural address, reprinted below, was delivered to a large outdoor audience in the nation's capitol on January 21, 1961. Kennedy set the tone and direction of his administration in a style that displayed the qualities of effectiveness discussed in this chapter. The figures of speech and strategies of arrangement strengthened the impact of the ideas on the audience. As you read the speech, note especially the clarity and vividness given to ideas through careful construction of sentences.

1. Vice President Johnson, Mr. Speaker, Mr. Chief Justice, President Eisenhower, Vice President Nixon, President Truman, Reverend Clergy, Fellow Citizens: We observe today not a victory of party but a celebration of freedom—symbolizing an end as well as a beginning—

signifying renewal as well as change. For I have sworn before you and Almighty God the same solemn oath our forebears prescribed nearly a century and three quarters ago.

2. The world is very different now. For man holds in his mortal hands the power to abolish all forms of human poverty and all forms of human life. And yet the same revolutionary beliefs for which our forebears fought are still at issue around the globe—the belief that the rights of man come not from the generosity of the state but from the hand of God.

3. We dare not forget today that we are the heirs of that first revolution. Let the word go forth from this time and place, to friend and foe alike, that the torch has been passed to a new generation of Americans—born in this century, tempered by war, disciplined by a hard and bitter peace, proud of our ancient heritage—and unwilling to witness or permit the slow undoing of those human rights to which this nation has always been committed, and to which we are committed today, at home and around the world.

4. Let every nation know, whether it wishes us well or ill, that we shall pay any price, bear any burden, meet any hardship, support any friend or oppose any foe to assure the survival and the success of liberty.

5. This much we pledge—and more.

6. To those old allies whose cultural and spiritual origins we share, we pledge the loyalty of faithful friends. United, there is little we cannot do in a host of cooperative ventures. Divided, there is little we can do—for we dare not meet a powerful challenge at odds and split asunder.

7. To those new states whom we welcome to the ranks of the free, we pledge our word that one form of colonial control shall not have passed away merely to be replaced by a far more iron tyranny. We shall not always expect to find them supporting our view.

8. But we shall always hope to find them strongly supporting their own freedom—and to remember that, in the past, those who foolishly sought power by riding the back of the tiger ended up inside.

9. To those people in the huts and villages of half the globe struggling to break the bonds of mass misery, we pledge our best efforts to help them help themselves, for whatever period is required—not because the Communists may be doing it, not because we seek their votes, but because it is right. If a free society cannot help the many who are poor, it cannot save the few who are rich.

10. To our sister republics south of our border, we offer a special pledge—to convert our good words into good deeds—in a new alliance for progress—to assist free men and free governments in casting off the chains of poverty. But this peaceful revolution of hope cannot become the prey of hostile powers. Let all our neighbors know that we

shall join with them to oppose aggression or subversion anywhere in the Americas. And let every other power know that this hemisphere intends to remain the master of its own house.

11. To that world assembly of sovereign states, the United Nations, our last best hope in an age where the instruments of war have far outpaced the instruments of peace, we renew our pledge of support—to prevent it from becoming merely a forum for invective—to strengthen its shield of the new and the weak—and to enlarge the area in which its writ may run.

12. Finally, to those nations who would make themselves our adversary, we offer not a pledge but a request: That both sides begin anew the quest for peace, before the dark powers of destruction unleashed by science engulf all humanity in planned or accidental self-destruction.

13. We dare not tempt them with weakness. For only when our arms are sufficient beyond doubt can we be certain beyond doubt that they will never be employed.

14. But neither can two great and powerful groups of nations take comfort from our present course—both sides overburdened by the cost of modern weapons, both rightly alarmed by the steady spread of the deadly atom, yet both racing to alter that uncertain balance of terror that stays the hand of mankind's final war.

15. So let us begin anew—remembering on both sides that civility is not a sign of weakness, and sincerity is always subject to proof. Let us never negotiate out of fear. But let us never fear to negotiate.

16. Let both sides explore what problems unite us instead of belaboring those problems which divide us.

17. Let both sides, for the first time, formulate serious and precise proposals for the inspection and control of arms—and bring the absolute power to destroy other nations under the absolute control of all nations.

18. Let both sides seek to invoke the wonders of science instead of its terrors. Together let us explore the stars, conquer the deserts, eradicate disease, tap the ocean depths and encourage the arts and commerce.

19. Let both sides unite to heed in all corners of the earth the command of Isaiah—to "undo the heavy burdens . . . [and] let the oppressed go free."

20. And if a beachhead of cooperation may push back the jungle of suspicion, let both sides join in creating a new endeavor: not a new balance of power, but a new world of law, where the strong are just and the weak secure and the peace preserved.

21. All this will not be finished in the first one hundred days. Nor will it be finished in the first one thousand days, nor in the life of this administration, nor even perhaps in our lifetime on this planet. But let us begin.

22. In your hands, my fellow citizens, more than mine, will rest the final success or failure of our course. Since this country was founded, each generation of Americans has been summoned to give testimony to its national loyalty. The graves of young Americans who answered the call to service surround the globe.

23. Now the trumpet summons us again—not as a call to bear arms, though arms we need—not as a call to battle, though embattled we are—but a call to bear the burden of a long twilight struggle, year in and year out, "rejoicing in hope, patient in tribulation"—a struggle against the common enemies of man: Tyranny, poverty, disease and war itself.

24. Can we forge against these enemies a grand and global alliance, North and South, East and West, that can assure a more fruitful life for all mankind? Will you join in that historic effort?

25. In the long history of the world, only a few generations have been granted the role of defending freedom in its hour of maximum danger.

26. I do not shrink from this responsibility—I welcome it. I do not believe that any of us would exchange places with any other people or any other generation. The energy, the faith, the devotion which we bring to this endeavor will light our country and all who serve it—and the glow from that fire can truly light the world.

27. And so, my fellow Americans: Ask not what your country can do for you—ask what you can do for your country.

28. My fellow citizens of the world: Ask not what America will do for you, but what together we can do for the freedom of man.

29. Finally, whether you are citizens of America or citizens of the world, ask of us here the same high standards of strength and sacrifice which we ask of you. With a good conscience our only sure reward, with history the final judge of our deeds, let us go forth to lead the land we love, asking His blessing and His help, but knowing that here on earth God's work must truly be our own.[45]

EXERCISES

UTILIZATION

16. Analyze the use of style in the preceding Inaugural Address by John F. Kennedy. In your essay, you should evaluate the qualities of style reflected, the use of figures of speech, and the use of strategies for arranging ideas.

UTILIZATION

17. Construct a two-minute speech using careful word choice, at least five figures of speech, and at least two strategies for arranging ideas.

Notes

1. John F. Wilson and Carroll C. Arnold, *Public Speaking as a Liberal Art,* 2d ed. (Boston, Mass.: Allyn and Bacon, 1968), p. 288.

2. Harry S. Truman, *Truman Speaks* (New York: Columbia University Press, 1960), p. 35.

3. Stokely Carmichael in Robert L. Scott and Wayne Brockriede, *The Rhetoric of Black Power* (New York: Harper and Row, 1969), p. 87.

4. Ibid., p. 99.

5. Ross Smyth, "Humour (Or Humor) in Public Speaking," *Vital Speeches* 40 (1 September 1974): 691.

6. Gerald Ford, "The Economy," *Vital Speeches* 40 (1 September 1974): 676.

7. Gerald Goldhaber, "Organizational Communication," *Vital Speeches* 42 (15 February 1976): 270.

8. Dr. Jerome Kagen, "The Dissolution of Basic Values," *Vital Speeches* 39 (15 July, 1973): 603.

9. Leslie Pagel, Unpublished Manuscript, University of Wisconsin, 1974.

10. Senator George Vest, *Indianapolis News,* 12 September 1924, p. 6.

11. Oliver Jensen, "And Now for a Few Closing Remarks by President Eisenhower." Copyright © Oliver Jensen 1957.

12. Jane Blankenship, *Public Speaking: A Rhetorical Perspective* (Englewood Cliffs, N.J.: Prentice Hall, 1966), pp. 101–02.

13. Adlai Stevenson, "Sir Winston Churchill," *Washington Post,* 29 January 1965, p. A5.

14. Martin Luther King, Jr., "I Have a Dream." Reprinted by permission of Joan Daves. Copyright © 1963 by Martin Luther King, Jr.

15. Robert W. Swinarton, "The Outlook for Our Capital Markets," *Vital Speeches* 42 (1 February 1976): 256.

16. Alexander M. Schmidt, "Great Expectations," *Vital Speeches* 42 (1 March 1976): 306.

17. Charles N. Kimball, "Renaissance or Ruin?" *Vital Speeches* 42 (15 January 1976): 199.

18. Jack Anderson, "How Washington Laughs at Itself," *Parade Magazine* (5 February 1967).

19. Jenkin L. Jones, "Let's Bring Back Dad," *Vital Speeches* 39 (15 May 1973): 473.

20. Marie Ransley, "The Life and Death of Our Lakes," in Wil Linkugel, R. R. Allen, and R. Johannesen, *Contemporary American Speeches,* 3d ed. (Belmont, Cal.: Wadsworth Publishing Co., 1972), p. 66 (Emphasis added).

21. Gerald Krause, Unpublished Manuscript, University of Wisconsin, 1974.

22. King, "Dream." Reprinted by permission of Joan Daves. Copyright © 1973 by Martin Luther King, Jr.

23. John F. Kennedy, "The Intellectual and the Politician," in Wil Linkugel, R. R. Allen, and R. Johannesen, *Contemporary American Speeches* (Belmont, Cal.: Wadsworth Publishing Co., 1965), p. 281.

24. Ina Brownlee Bragdon, "A Plea for Migrant Children," *Vital Speeches* 40 (1 September 1974): 695–99.

25. Krause, Unpublished Manuscript, University of Wisconsin, 1974.

26. Martin Luther King, Jr. "Love, Law, and Civil Disobedience," in Linkugel, *American Speeches,* 3d ed., p. 81.

27. Jerome Kagen, "The Dissolution of Basic Values," *Vital Speeches* 39 (15 July 1973): p. 603.

28. Robert V. Andelson, "Campus Unrest: The Erosion of Excellence," *Vital Speeches* 36 (1 August 1970), 619.

29. William Pinson, "The Playboy Philosophy—Con," in Linkugel, *American Speeches,* 3rd ed., pp. 176–178.

30. Felipe V. Ponce, Jr., "La Causa," in Linkugel et al., *American Speeches,* 3d ed., p. 67.

31. Adlai Stevenson, "Let Us Work While It Is Yet Day," in Linkugel et al., *American Speeches,* p. 288.

32. Spiro Agnew, Speech Delivered to State Republican Convention, San Diego, California, 11 September 1970, in James M. Naughton, "Agnew Aims Fire at G.O.P. Liberals," *New York Times,* 12 September 1970, p. 7.

33. Jane Blankenship, *Public Speaking: A Rhetorical Perspective* (Englewood Cliffs, N.J.: Prentice-Hall, 1966), pp. 133–34.

34. Douglas MacArthur, "Farewell to the Cadets," in Linkugel, *American Speeches,* 3d ed., p. 286.

35. Elizabeth Langer, "An Instrument of Revelation," in Linkugel, *American Speeches,* 3d ed., pp. 300–301.

36. King, "Dream." Reprinted by Permission of Joan Daves. Copyright © 1973 by Martin Luther King, Jr.

37. Adlai Stevenson, "Sir Winston Churchill," *Washington Post,* 29 January 1965, p. A5.

38. Ponce, "La Causa," in Linkugel, *American Speeches,* 3d ed., pp. 69–70.

39. Sydney Smith, Speech given at the University of Toronto, in Donald C. Bryant and Karl R. Wallace, *Fundamentals of Public Speaking,* 4th ed. (New York: Appleton-Century-Crofts, 1969), p. 213.

40. Pinson, Jr., "Playboy—Con.," in Linkugel et al., *American Speeches,* 3d ed., p. 175.

41. King, "Dream." Reprinted by permission of Joan Daves. Copyright © 1973 by Martin Luther King, Jr.

42. Andelson, "Campus Unrest," *Vital Speeches* 36:619.

43. MacArthur, "Cadets," in Linkugel et al., *American Speeches,* 3d ed., p. 286.

44. King, "Dream." Reprinted by permission of Joan Daves. Copyright © 1973 by Martin Luther King, Jr.

45. John F. Kennedy, "Inaugural Address, 1961," in *Public Papers of the Presidents: John F. Kennedy, 1961* (Washington, D.C.: Government Printing office, 1962), pp. 1–3.

4

organization

learning objectives

Recall
Comprehension
Application
Analysis
Synthesis

By the conclusion of this chapter you will be able to:

1. Identify the names of nine patterns of organization.

2. Match the names of organizational patterns with their definitions.

3. Identify the organizational patterns employed in sample outlines.

4. Determine which patterns of organization were used in sample speeches.

5. Identify six functions commonly assigned to speech introductions.

6. Select descriptions of the six functions of introductions from a list of responses.

7. Identify five devices commonly used in speech conclusions.

8. Match terms for concluding devices with definitions of such devices.

9. Identify sample introductory and concluding devices by type.

10. Determine which devices are being used in sample introductions and conclusions.

11. Construct an introduction that serves all six functions and a conclusion that includes at least three devices.

12. Identify four guidelines for refining the speech outline.

13. Match guidelines for refining the speech outline with guideline definitions.

14. Unscramble a scrambled outline that includes at least one level of subordination.

15. Identify statements in a sample outline that violate the guidelines.

16. Construct an outline consistent with the guidelines.

> Socrates: Well, there is one point at least which I think you will admit, namely that any discourse ought to be constructed like a living creature, with its own body, as it were; it must not lack either head or feet; it must have a middle and extremities so composed as to suit each other and the whole work.
>
> Plato's *Phaedrus*

Whenever two or more college instructors assemble these days, the topic of conversation eventually turns to the subject of how poorly students write. Although this criticism is prompted partially by student misspellings, errant syntax, and impoverished vocabulary, the major thrust of criticism is directed at the alleged inability of students to identify a crucial issue with precision and to order their thoughts in such a way that the issue is logically and sufficiently developed.

Does this criticism apply to you? Have you received a corrected paper lately on which an instructor has scribbled, "get to the point," "sharpen your focus," "repetitious," "disorganized," "cluttered," or "fuzzy"? When did one of your instructors last observe, "incisive," "superbly structured," "nicely developed," "thorough," "a competent analysis," or "may I have a copy of this paper?"

In the headnote to this chapter, Plato, writing twenty-four centuries ago, captured the essence of effective organization. In the following pages you will be encouraged to perfect your organizational skills along the general lines that Plato suggested. Although we are primarily interested in ordering ideas for delivery in public contexts, the skills that you will sharpen are relevant to the essay as well as to the speech.

This chapter will be developed in three sections: organizing the body of the speech, preparing introductions and conclusions, and refining the speech outline.

Organizing the Body of the Speech

In this section we will consider nine patterns of organization that speakers have found useful in unfolding their ideas. As you consider these patterns, keep two key questions in mind:

1. Does this pattern allow me to say what I want to say about my subject?
2. Does this pattern invite audience involvement in the unfolding of my ideas?

We hope that as you read this section you will begin to think creatively about the ways in which you can organize the ideas that are important to you.

Chronological Pattern

Chronology refers to the arrangement of events in the order of their occurrence. The chronological pattern is useful in describing events that have occurred over a period of time or processes that require a sequence of steps or stages. Speeches that recall America's heritage, recount the fall of former President Nixon, or review the growth of the women's liberation movement are potential candidates for a chronological development. When considering *historical events,* the chronology enables audiences to perceive crucial moments in time as they are influenced by earlier events and as they influence events that follow. A historical narrative can exert a powerful emotional force upon an audience. Franklin Delano Roosevelt, in his Declaration of War Speech observed:

> The attack yesterday on the Hawaiian Islands has caused severe damage to American naval and military forces. Very many American lives have been lost. In addition, American ships have been reported torpedoed on the high seas between San Francisco and Honolulu.
> Last night Japanese forces attacked Hong Kong.
> Last night Japanese forces attacked Guam.
> Last night Japanese forces attacked Wake Island.
> This morning the Japanese attacked Midway Island.[1]

Why did F.D.R. order this section of his speech chronologically—"yesterday," "last night," "this morning"? What effect would this order have on an audience already stunned by "the day that will live in infamy"? It suggests, does it not, that the Japanese attack was a calculated, ongoing event that showed promise of continuing.

If your purpose is to explain a *process or procedure* to your audience, temporal order may be merely helpful or absolutely crucial. Consider the implications for chronological development in such topics as applying for financial aid, combining chemicals in a laboratory experiment, giving mouth-to-mouth resuscitation, executing a complicated zone defense, introducing a marketing strategy for a new product, or establishing a small business. In each of these cases, the audience can check their progress toward accomplishment of the task by reviewing the steps presented. Chronological organization may be imperative, as in the case of explaining mouth-to-mouth resuscitation, when the audience must accomplish one step before it can proceed to the next.

The two examples that follow demonstrate how the chronological pattern may be used to organize the main ideas of speeches.

Subject: U.S. Involvement in Vietnam
Purpose: To explain the extent of U.S. involvement in Vietnamese affairs from a historical perspective
Main Points:
I. U.S. involvement began during the Eisenhower and Kennedy administrations.
II. U.S. involvement dramatically escalated during the Johnson and Nixon years.
III. U.S. involvement dramatically terminated during the late Nixon and Ford years.

Subject: Videotaping in the Classroom
Purpose: To describe the procedure for videotaping in the classroom setting
Main Points:
I. The videotape equipment must be properly stationed.
II. The videotape recording process consists of four essential steps.
III. The videotape playback process consists of three essential steps.

In the first instance, the chronological pattern was used to provide historical perspective. In the second instance, it was used to describe the major aspects of a procedure.

Spatial Pattern

If someone asks you for directions, the response you give undoubtedly will be organized in terms of the physical relationships of objects in space: "Go down this street to the first light; turn left; and it's the purple house just past the one painted bright orange. *You can't miss it.*" In a similar fashion, you might describe the services of your library in spatial terms: "On the first floor, we have . . . ; on the second floor, you will find. . . ." Once you have selected the starting point, the remaining points follow systematically. A speech explaining the location of mineral deposits might proceed in terms of elevation (sea level to 1500 feet, 1500 feet to 3000 feet) or by geographical region (northwestern states, southwestern states).

In addition to describing and explaining, spatial order also may heighten the persuasive impact of your message. You may organize a speech on strip-mining by geographic region and gain nothing from the pattern but clarity. However, with apt use of language you can make the pattern work for you in involving the audience: "As we examine the eastern states, the harsh reality of a despoiled America becomes apparent. . . . The giant scoop shovels, in their insatiable hunger, also have left telltale tooth marks throughout the plains of mid-America. . . . Even the great natural beauty of the West has not been spared." As you progress from region to region, you create the impression of a whole nation senselessly scoured by the mighty machines of the quick-profit ethic.

The sample outline that follows demonstrates the use of a spatial pattern in organizing a speech on Disney World.

Subject: Disney World
Purpose: To describe the six glorious lands of Walt Disney's Magic Kingdom

I. We begin the journey on Main Street, U.S.A.
II. Moving clockwise, we enter the wide world of Adventureland.
III. Next, we encounter the primitive life of Frontierland.
IV. In Liberty Square we relive important moments in American history.
V. In Fantasy Land every adult again becomes a child.
VI. Before completing the circle at Main Street, we are catapulted into the wonders of Tomorrowland.

In this example, the spatial pattern is used to chart a course through the maze of one of America's most popular tourist attractions.

Rank-Order Pattern

Speakers sometimes organize their ideas in terms of importance or strength. Two common rank-order patterns are:

Ascending order: the arrangement of ideas from least to most important or from weakest to strongest.
Descending order: the arrangement of ideas from most to least important or strongest to weakest.

Rank-ordering patterns require that you make judgments about the relative importance or strength of your ideas.

These patterns can be used to achieve a number of speech purposes. Imagine that you wish to *inform* your audience about alternative sources of energy. Since oil and natural gas resources are becoming increasingly scarce and expensive, you may believe that it is important that the audience understand the relative potential of various alternative resources for contributing to the energy pool. If so, a rank-order pattern such as the following would be appropriate:

Subject: Alternative Sources of Energy
Purpose: To inform the audience about alternative energy resources

I. The harnessing of natural energy (tides and winds) will require extensive research and development.
II. Solar energy holds substantial promise.
III. Nuclear energy has the greatest immediate potential.

In this instance, an ascending order is used to differentiate among energy alternatives.

Rank-order patterns also may be used in speeches with a *persuasive* purpose. The following example of a descending order pertains:

Subject: Environmental Pollution
Purpose: To convince the audience that environmental pollution requires urgent attention

I. Air pollution has reached staggering proportions.
II. Water pollution is becoming a critical problem.
III. Noise pollution is more than merely bothersome.

Does it make a difference whether you present these arguments in ascending or descending order? Recent research indicates that the ascending order may be the most effective if your goal is to have the audience remember your most important point; the assumption is that the last idea your audience is exposed to will be retained longest. This research is inconclusive with respect to the influence of order differences on attitude change.

Refutative Pattern

This pattern organizes a speech in terms of opposing arguments and is most appropriate in persuasive settings. A student recently used this pattern successfully in a speech favoring sex education:

Subject: Sex Education in the Schools
Purpose: To convince the audience that the arguments of the opponents of sex education have no merit

I. The argument of the sex education opponents that there is no need for sex education programs is wrong.
II. The argument that increased exposure to sex-related topics will lead to increased promiscuity is patently false.
III. The argument that sex education is better provided privately in the home and the church is naïve.[2]

In this instance, the student built his case by refuting common objections to sex education programs. This pattern of organization can be very persuasive with an audience that is somewhat sympathetic to the speaker's position. It invites the audience to share in the psychological destruction of unpopular arguments.

Problem-Solution Pattern

As its title implies, this pattern subdivides the body of a speech into two sections: (1) the *problem* being discussed and (2) the *solution* or alternative solutions that would alleviate or cure the problem. Each of the sections—problem and solution—requires additional organizational patterns for its development.

Dianne Klemme, who won first place in the 1970 Interstate Oratorical Association Contest (Women's Division) provided an excellent example of the problem-solution pattern. An adapted outline of her speech follows:

Subject: The Age of Gerontion
Purpose: To convince the audience that changes must be made in our perceptions of the aged

I. Problem: Popular societal perceptions are destructive.
  A. General societal perceptions are destructive.
  B. The family's perceptions are destructive.
  C. The perceptions of the aged themselves are destructive.
II. Solution: A program for changing perceptions must be adopted.
  A. The aged must seek new options in living.
  B. We, as the nation's young, must ensure new options for our own age of gerontion.[3]

This pattern is especially effective when enlisting audience support for new courses of action. The first half of the speech invites the audience to empathize with those who are suffering: "Oh, isn't it dreadful how poorly we treat old people." The second half of the speech then enables the audience to effect psychological closure: "Well, I'm glad there's something constructive we can do about it."

Alternative Pattern

In a complex world, there are seldom single explanations of phenomena, single causes of problems, or single solutions to matters of social urgency. Whether the purpose is to inform or persuade, the alternative pattern is often a viable option.

When you wish to inform your audience, the alternative pattern enables you to examine a phenomenon from a number of different perspectives. For example, if you wish your audience to understand the nature of UFOs, you might present three or four discrete interpretations of what they are. Or, if you wish an audience to understand that insidious phenomenon "inflation," you might provide a number of different economic definitions or explanations. The alternative pattern enables your audience to compare different explanations of complex phenomena.

This pattern is used often in persuasive speeches advocating a particular course of action. To convince the audience that your course of action is best, you may first discredit the major competing courses of action. A. F. Arpaia, Vice-president of International Services of the Railway Express Agency, used this technique to pave the way for his solution to the problem of long, costly strikes in the transportation industry. A condensed outline of his speech illustrates this pattern:

Subject: Strikes in the Transportation Industry
Purpose: To convince the audience that binding arbitration is the best course of action

I. One alternative is the outright permanent ban against strikes, of any kind, in transportation.
   A. This has caused violence in the past.
   B. It coerces only one side.
   C. It ignores political reality.
II. Another alternative is administrative wage determination by the government itself.
   A. This is abhorrent to the free enterprise system.
   B. It wastes resources.
   C. It creates unwieldy bureaucracy
III. A third alternative is seizure by the government.
   A. This is the worst kind of government intervention.
   B. It creates problems of compensation.
IV. A fourth alternative is to apply antitrust laws to unions.
   A. Labor is not the same as business and should not be treated as such.
   B. The application would prove ineffectual.
V. A final alternative is some form of binding arbitration.
   A. This solution is preferred since all obstacles can be met.
   B. It is not "compulsory."
   C. It avoids problems through an independent tribunal.

D. It is compatible with the free enterprise system.
E. It does not eliminate collective bargaining.
F. Stalemates should not end in strikes.[4]

Instead of selecting a single solution and advancing it, Mr. Arpaia considered it expedient to first present and discard major alternatives. The acceptability of his solution (binding arbitration) was enhanced by the impression that this was the only practical remaining solution.

Causal Pattern

Whether you describe a cause to effect progression of events or relate effects and establish their causes, this pattern focuses attention on the interrelationship of events. Does the audience require knowledge of the causes of a specific problem? Is the link between current conditions and their causes an important or crucial one in supporting your position? Does your proposal boast that those factors producing the problem will be eliminated? In each of these instances, a "yes" response implies the appropriateness of a casual pattern.

Charles Schaillol, a student at Indiana University,[5] utilized an effects/cause pattern in convincing his audience that the automobile is the major cause of air pollution. After identifying and elaborating the major effects of pollution (death, accidents, and property damage), he asked, "What is the cause of such massive air contamination?" then followed the question with the argument that the automobile has surpassed industry as the most significant producer of pollution. The author's initial discussion of effects gave urgency to the search for a cause.

The sample outline that follows illustrates the use of a cause-effect pattern.

Subject: Sexism in School Textbooks
Purpose: To convince the audience that sexism in textbooks has dangerous social side effects

I. Sexism in school textbooks is widespread.
   A. Elementary school reading primers place women in inferior stereotypic roles.
   B. Intermediate elementary school textual materials relegate women to subservient positions in society.
   C. Secondary school textbooks show men on the cutting edge of society while women are neglected or relegated to positions of lesser importance.
II. The effects of these perspectives are socially disadvantageous.

A. Female high-school graduates have lower career expectations than male graduates.
B. Female high-school graduates have a lower image of self-worth than male high-school graduates.

This pattern highlights the relationship between sexism in textbooks and female self-perception. As with all causal arguments, this example should invite careful questioning, (are there other causes for the effects being cited?).

The Comparison/Contrast Pattern

How do you sell a Datsun to a person who expresses an interest in a Ford Pinto? How do you convince a board of directors that your marketing strategy is better than the one they are currently using? The comparison/contrast approach allows you to focus the audience's attention on similarities and differences, or on advantages and disadvantages of competing products or proposals. It is also useful in speeches that highlight pro and con positions on significant questions. For example, imagine that you wish to provide your audience with information about the controversy that surrounded the landing of supersonic transports (SSTs) at major U. S. airports. Two comparison/contrast strategies are available to you:

Format A

Subject: SST Landings at U.S. Airports
Purpose: To inform the audience of pro and con positions regarding SST landings at U.S. airports

I. Are SSTs too noisy?
 A. The proponents say no.
 B. The opponents say yes.
II. Do SSTs pose a danger to health?
 A. The proponents say no.
 B. The opponents say yes.
III. Do SSTs pose a danger to safety?
 A. The proponents say no.
 B. The opponents say yes.

Format B

Subject and purpose: Same

I. The major arguments of the proponents are:
 A. Issue 1

B. Issue 2
C. Issue 3
II. The major arguments of the opponents are:
A. Issue 1
B. Issue 2
C. Issue 3

The above formats have respective strengths and weaknesses. Format A clearly identifies the differences with regard to specific questions but does not present a unified portrayal of either position. Format B offers a unified portrayal of each position at the expense of a clear illustration of differences.

Your choice of format will be influenced by which of these strengths would answer your particular needs. If, instead of informing your audience, you propose to refute one side's position, then format A would seem to be the most effective. If the audience is confused about who supports what, then format B may be more appropriate. One point to remember—this pattern requires additional organization; the development of ideas under each main point must be arranged chronologically, topically, by rank-order, or by some other approach.

The Topical Pattern

When the main points emerge as special topics of the subject matter in question and when other patterns are inapplicable, a topical pattern probably is most appropriate. Two types of topical patterns can be distinguished: (1) logical progression and (2) random ordering.

Logical progression. Arranging a discussion of welfare costs by reference to local, county, state, and national agencies is an example of logical progression. Discussing alternative church budgets in terms of their respective amounts ("bare bones," "growth," and "ideal") is another example. Subjects such as population growth or production of oil might be subdivided into national and international, with the latter further divided into geographic regions. The distinguishing feature in each of these instances is that a particular standard (size, scope, cost) is used to arrange the topics.

Random ordering. In random ordering, the order of the topics can be interchanged without violating any natural logical progression. Martin Luther King, Jr., used this pattern in discussing the central, identifying features of the civil disobedience movement. The topics, in their order of development, were:

Subject: The Civil Disobedience Movement
Purpose: To explain the central features of civil disobedience

I. It is "based on the philosophy that ends and means must cohere."
II. Those who adhere to it "must follow a consistent principle of noninjury."
III. The movement seeks to defeat the system, not individuals.
IV. Suffering can be a "creative and powerful social force."
V. "Within human nature, there is an amazing potential for goodness." [6]

King's actual transitions between ideas would make it difficult to transpose paragraphs in the final version. However, there is nothing present in the initial development that would prohibit a reordering of the topics presented.

In this section, nine common patterns of organization have been discussed. Whichever patterns you may use, it is important that your audience senses an inherent logic to the unfolding of your ideas.

EXERCISES

VERIFICATION

1. Identify the nine patterns of organization.

VERIFICATION

2. Identify the pattern of organization that matches each of the following definitions. (Caution: two of the definitions do not apply.)

   a. ______________________ may concentrate on why an event occurred and indicate its consequences.

b. ______________________ evaluates a subject in terms of importance or strength of idea.

c. ______________________ examines the issue and offers a remedy.

d. ______________________ orders ideas in time sequence.

e. ______________________ tears down the opposing position.

f. ______________________ offers a classical approach to the arrangement of ideas.

g. ______________________ orders ideas in terms of physical relationships.

h. ______________________ may arrange by a type of logical progression.

i. ______________________ explores a subject by examining available options.

j. ______________________ organizes in terms of problem and proof.

k. ______________________ arranges on a basis of similarities and differences.

UTILIZATION

3. Examine each of the following sample outlines. If the elements are in proper order, simply label the pattern being represented. If the outline needs rearranging, indicate the new order (number items 1, 2, etc.) and label the new pattern.

a. Subject: President Nixon's Pardon

_____ The argument that Nixon should have been pardoned because he was ill is without merit.

_____ The argument that Nixon should have been pardoned because of "presidential privilege" is without merit.

_____ The argument that Nixon should have been pardoned because he suffered enough is without merit.

Pattern______________________

b. Subject: American Foreign Policy

_____ America is reluctant to engage in foreign military engagements.

_____ America has suffered stalemates or defeats in its major military involvements since World War II.

Pattern______________________

c. Subject: United States Time Zones

_____ Mountain

_____ Eastern

_____ Pacific

_____ Atlantic

_____ Central

Pattern_____________________________

d. Subject: Major American Political Philosophies

_____ The conservative favors the preservation of established institutions, the capitalistic system, and minimum government interference in the affairs of citizens.

_____ The liberal favors change in established institutions, approves of capitalism but stresses the rights of the worker, and favors massive governmental programs as solutions to social problems.

Pattern_____________________________

e. Subject: Mouth-to-Mouth Resuscitation

_____ Blow gently.

_____ Tilt chin upward.

_____ Keep repeating the preceding two steps.

_____ Dislodge tongue or foreign matter from throat.

_____ Press firmly on victim's chest to force air out.

_____ Place your mouth over victim's mouth.

Pattern_____________________________

f. Subject: The Plight of the American Indian

_____ All Americans of Indian lineage should be guaranteed a minimum living wage.

_____ American Indians suffer lower incomes, shorter lives, greater unemployment, and lower living standards than any other segment of the American population.

Pattern_____________________________

g. Subject: Patterns of Organization

_____ Causal

_____ Problem-Solution

_____ Rank Order

_____ Chronological

_____ Spatial

_____ Alternative

_____ Refutative

_____ Topical

_____ Comparison/Contrast

Pattern_____________________________

h. Subject: Hypotheses regarding UFO's

_____ UFOs are really the product of alien planets.

_____ UFOs are nothing more than optical illusions.

_____ UFOs are military spy ships from other countries.

_____ UFO's are figments of the imaginations of "crazies."

Pattern_____________________________

i. Subject: Standard Measurements Used In American Cooking (From Large to Small).

_____ Gallon

_____ Pinch

_____ Teaspoon

_____ Pint

_____ Quart

_____ Tablespoon

_____ Cup

Pattern_____________________________

UTILIZATION

4. Analyze the three speech fragments that follow. At the conclusion of each quotation, identify (a) the major points of the passage and (b) the pattern of organization represented.

a. . . . we might divide . . . discriminatory laws into three categories. . . . There are laws which are still on the books in many states which resemble archaic remnants of the federal coverture law in which a married woman's legal responsibilities were covered by her husband. She had none. . . . We find laws which are a sort of "back-handed compliment" to women. She is supposed to be of a higher order of virtue than the male. For example, many states require that a woman convicted of a crime be sentenced differently and generally more severely than a man. . . . This same assumption of a woman's higher virtue shows up in the double sex standard. In Oakland two prostitutes are appealing. They were convicted, but their clients were released. . . .

A third group of discriminatory laws are those which were designed to protect women as fragile creatures but actually hurt them economically. Many state laws prohibit women from working at night—which in effect prevents them from getting overtime.[7]

1. Major points:

2. Pattern:

b. Throughout the history of the United States, seapower has been an integral part in making this nation great. . . . On 13 October 1775 the Continental Congress authorized the acquisition and construction of ships for the Continental Navy. . . . The War of 1812 was fought ostensibly to defend the doctrine of "freedom of the seas". . . . In 1890 RADM Alfred Thayer published his internationally famous work, *The Influence of Sea Power on History*. . . . President Roosevelt put sea power into action. The Spanish American War had projected the United States into the role of a world power with overseas interests and territories requiring a strong Navy. In 1907 he sent his famous "Great White Fleet" on a two-year, around-the-world cruise. . . . There is no doubt that seapower has played an integral role in the development of this country.[8]

1. Major points:

2. Pattern:

c. I want to tell you about longtime friends, former students, and casual acquaintances who exemplify their respective 20th century cultures. Let's begin our "great race" with a visit to Pedro, a farmer in Mexico. . . . Pedro is about 60 and rents his 5 acres from an absentee landlord. . . . Let's hop across Central America to Peru. Here is Rafael from a traditional Peruvian family with origins going back several hundred years. . . . Across the south Atlantic is Algeria which became independent of France in 1962. About a tenth of the farm land has

> been "socialized" into government cooperatives. . . . Let's move now across the Mediterranean to the Netherlands where a 40 year old Dutch businessman—we'll call him Derek—works for the telephone company in Amsterdam. . . . Our journey hastens on for a short stop at Saudi Arabia, a leader among the oil-producing nations and the one which has just "bought out" or expropriated, however you see it, the Aramco Corporation. . . . And now on to India where our friend Mehta is in his field. . . . Our around the world junket could go on, but it is time to draw some conclusions. . . .[9]

1. Major points:

2. Pattern:

Preparing Introductions and Conclusions

Having completed the body of the speech, the novice speaker is convinced that the task is finished. The speech may simply begin, "Today, I'm going to talk about. . . ." and end with something like, "Well, . . . I guess that's about it, folks." Experienced speakers know that such is not the case.

The introduction and the conclusion are vital parts of the speech and deserve the same kind of careful consideration that you have given to the major development of your ideas. In this section, you will be asked to consider six functions that an introduction may serve. You will then be invited to consider five devices that speakers frequently use in bringing their speeches to effective conclusions.

Introductions

A good introduction may accomplish a number of things: it may capture the attention of the audience; it may help to build your credibility; it may convince the audience that the subject is important; it may provide essential background information; it may clarify your speech purpose; and it may let the audience know how you intend to proceed. Each of these functions will be considered in turn.

Statements to focus attention. The first few seconds of a speech are very important. The bumbling, fumbling, inept speaker soon convinces an audience that they have little reason to attend to the message. So, too, does the speaker who begins each speech with an irrelevant and unfunny story (the same one each time). The speaker's opening remarks should arrest the attention of the audience and direct it to the rhetorical event that is about to unfold. There are, of course, a number of ways to do this.

A startling statement has the effect of shocking the audience or of arousing their curiosity. Consider the impact of the following statements:

"I am a hemophiliac." [10]

"Warning: The green slime is here! ! !" [11]

A quotation, followed by a statement of its relevance to the subject, can capture the essence of your message. The first example also possesses shock value.

> "Frankly, my dear, I don't give a damn." This line, from *Gone with the Wind,* was hard won from the industry's censors by David Selznick in 1939. Now, thirty-five years later, this line would hardly be cause for concern.[12]

> "The reliance of our race upon the progress achievements of others for justice, and rights is like a dependence upon a broken stick, it will eventually consign you to the ground. . . . The negro needs a nation and a country of his own where he can best show evidence of his own ability in the art of human progress."
>
> Up until a few short years ago, relatively few negroes adhered to the concept of "Black Nationalism" alluded to in these words of Marcus Garvey, spoken nearly 50 years ago. Complete integration into American society was what most negroes wanted. Today, however, such is not the case.[13]

A reference to the audience lets the members of the audience know that you perceive them as a unique group of people. A carefully composed reference to the audience also may enable you to establish an easy rapport, as was the case when Thomas Peters of the Detroit Free Press addressed an audience of teachers in convention:

> Good morning. It is my pleasure to speak to you today on your "day off." As I remember it, this is the day when you get away from the kids, the classrooms, and teaching and take an opportunity to unwind, gather your thoughts, and then plan some new strategies to help you through your next lap of teaching—from October 13, today, until Thanksgiv-

> ing. Once you make it to Thanksgiving, you've got it made, because you can then practically coast into Christmas. My assignment today is a delightful one that I hardly hoped for when, as a child, I was the captive audience for innumerable parochial school teachers. Little did I think, as I sat in those endless classes and rattled off my spelling and catechism and arithmetic lessons, that some day I would face 800 teachers myself and thus be in the enviable position of having them captive of me for all of 45 minutes, and to make things even more delightful—to have a completely open door subject-wise.[14]

A direct reference to the subject, when carefully handled, also can heighten the audience's interest and attention. Speaking on the subject "Projected Surrender of the United States Canal Zone," David J. Flood, United States Representative from Pennsylvania, noted:

> The Panama Canal is the strategic center of the Western Hemisphere. As foreseen by Simon Bolivar, it shortens the distances of the world and strengthens the commercial ties of Europe, the Americas and Asia. Annually transiting about 15,000 vessels from some 55 countries with about 70 percent of its traffic either originating or terminating in the United States, it is truly the jugular vein of the Americas.[15]

A reference to the occasion lets the audience know that you understand the ceremonial requirements of the gathering and that you empathize with them on this particular occasion. James N. Sites, Special Assistant to the Secretary of the Treasury, expressed such recognition when he addressed the 1975 San Francisco State University commencement audience.

> It is a deep personal honor to appear before this great university and this graduating class. . . . You who have journeyed across the years to this milepost in your lives can be proud. . . . You deserve sincere congratulations on the achievement. And let me also extend these good wishes to your teachers, parents, families and friends—to all those who have helped you and shared in your endeavor.
>
> I know that your years have been filled with tumult and turbulence. One can hardly be blamed for recalling in this regard the words Bob Hope uttered on a similar occasion—"To you who are about to go forth into the world," he said, "I have one word of advice—DON'T." [16]

An illustration, either hypothetical or real, can enhance the interest value of your speech by making your subject personal, vivid, and of compelling social urgency. A student began a speech with this illustration:

> Joe, a 21 year old business student at Indiana University, came from a "nice" family. In the midst of working for his degree, he had several dates with twenty year old Nancy, an I.U. music student and also

from a "nice" family. During the course of their relationship, Nancy and Joe became infected with a disease that neither of them knew they had contracted—venereal disease.[17]

On another occasion, a student speaker introduced the subject of old age in the following manner:

> She turned seventy-five last December. A year ago her husband suffered a cerebral hemorrhage which crippled and killed him before my grandmother's shocked eyes. Now she lives alone in the house she shared with grandfather for half a century, economically independent, proud that she can provide for herself in these her later years. Yet her independence cannot compensate for the limited mobility which isolates her from family and friends. Her pride cannot quell the fear she experiences daily: fear of assault and robbery by someone tempted by her slow steps and faltering cane.[18]

An intriguing statement or rhetorical question can capture the attention of the audience and cause them to wish to hear more. A student speaker used this supposition to heighten interest in her topic when she said:

> Suppose you were to be told that the philodendron plant resting on your window sill screams silently whenever you crack an egg, or that the potted dracaena on the sun porch grows apprehensive whenever the dog goes by.[19]

In more direct fashion, another student focused attention on the plight of the American Indian with questions:

> How many of you ever considered *why* the Custer Massacre and the Battle of Wounded Knee? Now, I don't mean why these confrontations occurred historically. I do mean why the terms? Why these labels? [20]

The seven kinds of attention materials presented above are not intended to be exhaustive. Armed with your creative intellect and a year's supply of *Vital Speeches,* you could identify a number of other devices that speakers use.

Statements to enhance credibility. Centuries ago Aristotle noted that the speaker's character (ethos or credibility) "may almost be called the most effective means of persuasion he possesses." [21] We attend to, believe, and trust speakers who are qualified and demonstrate habits of character that we honor.

As you prepare your introduction, you should consider carefully the credibility that you hold for your audience and seek to enhance that credibility as the speech unfolds. The introduction to your speech provides an excellent opportunity for you to demonstrate that you are especially well-qualified to talk about the subject in question. Ralph Zimmerman not only captured attention through a startling statement; he also identified himself as one who has exceptional personal qualifications to speak:

> I am a hemophiliac. To many of you, that word signifies little or nothing. A few may pause a moment and then remember that it has something to do with bleeding. Probably none of you can appreciate the gigantic impact of what those words mean to me.[22]

Major Nick Rowe used self-reference to his advantage in establishing his knowledge of the life of a prisoner of war. He observed:

> The American prisoners of war are particularly close to those of us in the military, because the prisoners of war are members of the military. It could be any one of us, and I was one of those prisoners of war. I am Major Nick Rowe; I spent 62 months as a prisoner of the Viet Cong in South Vietnam.[23]

In both of these speeches, audience members are given the impression that the speaker certainly ought to know what he is talking about.

Student speakers may not rely on a long list of accomplishments that qualify them to speak on all great topics of public importance. Still, if you choose topics for your speeches that grow out of your past interests and experiences, and if you engage in careful additional research, you are something of an expert. Your task is to let your expertise show without seeming boastful. Your attempts to establish credibility may initially seem stilted and blatant. As you grow as a message strategist, you will learn to be subtle as you verify your competence to speak.

Statements of importance. There are three reasons why the importance or relevance of the topic should be made clear to your audience. First, the audience may be unaware of the topic's importance. A speech on the aged, delivered to teenagers, needs to overcome a natural apathetic reaction, as might a lecture on alcoholism to sixth graders. Felipe Ponce highlighted the relevance of knowledge about the Chicano movement for an audience of midwestern college students:

> There are other reasons why this movement should be understood. If you're interested in politics, nine million people are hard to ignore. If you're interested in social problems, nine million people are hard to ignore. If you're interested in business, a market of nine million people is hard to ignore.[24]

Second, the importance may be accepted, but the audience may feel that you represent the wrong side of the issue. Your task in a speech favoring abortion before a pro-life group is to give the audience reasons for hearing you out. Henry Grady faced this problem when he addressed a northern audience following the Civil War. Grady, a southern newspaper editor, rose to speak just as the audience finished a chorus of "Marching through Georgia." He observed:

> I ask an indulgent hearing from you. I beg that you will bring your full faith in American fairness and frankness to judgment on what I shall say.[25]

In the face of a hostile audience, a speaker may call upon cherished traditions and values in urging that his or her message receive a fair hearing.

Finally, even where the relevance is known and the audience is not hostile to you or to your position, you may choose to highlight your topic by showing its special significance. In attacking the news media, Spiro Agnew addressed the significance of his topic in these terms:

> No nation depends more on the intelligent judgment of its citizens. No medium has a more profound influence over public opinion. Nowhere in our system are there fewer checks on federal power.[26]

Regardless of your subject or audience, you are well-advised to consider the relationship between the two. If your introduction does not give the audience a reason to listen—they won't.

Statements providing background. Speakers often find it necessary to provide essential background information in the introductions to their speeches. Among the background materials included are definitions of key terms, statements of historical perspective, and the identification of the larger fabric of which the subject is a part. For example, Phyllis Jones Springen, in beginning her speech on "The Dimensions of the Oppression of Women," provided the following historical perspective:

> Two especially important pieces of legislation concerning women have been in Congress in the past six years. The first was Title VII of the Civil Rights Act of 1964, which prohibited discrimination in employment on the basis of race, color, religion, national origin, or *sex*. What most people don't know is that the word, "sex," was proposed by eighty-one year old Congressman Howard Smith of Virginia. We all remember Howard Smith, Chairman of the Rules Committee. He was no promoter of civil rights and certainly no feminist. His "little amendment," as he called it, was designed to defeat the bill. The bill passed, and although the provision for no discrimination on the basis of sex is not stringently enforced, it did lay the foundation of women's fight for equal employment.

> The second piece of legislation, which did not pass in the last session of Congress, was the proposed Equal Rights Amendment to the United States Constitution. It read: "Equality of rights under the law shall not be denied or abridged by the United States or any state on account of sex." The amendment failed to pass, possibly because most people are unaware of the tangle of laws all across the United States which discriminate against women.[27]

In this instance, Ms. Springen thought it important to review the status of recent legislation before talking about the glut of archaic discriminatory laws against women. As you consider your audience's knowledge of your subject, you may wish to include essential background material in your introduction.

Statements of subject or purpose. We once knew a minister who was a master of the art of unclear speaking. He spoke with incredible vocal and physical dynamism, used language that was rich with figurative adornment, and drew heavily from religious and secular literature in seeking to give his message great depth and substance. Unfortunately, we could never quite figure out what he was talking about. Somewhere in your past you have probably known such a person or persons.

A speech is a transient kind of phenomenon. It is here for a moment and then gone. If the central idea of the message escapes the listener, it is lost forever. It is for this reason that speakers often explicitly state their central subject or purpose. This may be done in a number of ways. Consider the following examples:

> Now, I have been asked to talk about the philosophy behind the student movement.[28]

> So this afternoon I would like to bring you . . . some insight into what an American prisoner of war lives through.[29]

> But I didn't come here to dwell on the present situation of small private colleges. You are all too painfully familiar with that. Rather, I came here to speak about a different and really far more important topic—Does the small private college have a future?[30]

> This afternoon I want to discuss with you some of the assumptions of the insurance industry, and their relevance to our contemporary, consumer-oriented society.[31]

However the subject or purpose statement is phrased, it functions to familiarize the audience with the central thrust of the speech that is to follow.

Statements of partition. In addition to offering a general statement of subject or purpose, many speakers have found it helpful to preview the major lines of development that will unfold during their speeches. This preview, often called an *initial partition,* provides the audience with an intellectual map of your speech. Donald W. Whitehead, Federal Co-Chairman of the Appalachian Regional Commission, in talking about the values of patriotic holidays, provided the preview that follows:

> . . . let us analyze Memorial Day—What it meant in my grandparents' day, in my parents' day, in my day, and what it may mean in my children's day.[32]

Similarly, Professor William G. Carleton ended the introduction to his speech, "Effective Speech in a Democracy," with this initial partition:

> . . . but there has been a deterioration in the intellectual content, in the literary style, and in the method of delivering speeches, even among those who by reputation stand in the first rank of contemporary oratory and speech.[33]

He then proceeded to consider each of these areas of decline.

A well-phrased statement of partition invites the audience to understand the internal structure of the speech. As the speech unfolds, the audience can find satisfaction in "knowing where they are."

Conclusion

The conclusion should end the speech in a forceful, fitting way. It should reemphasize the points that you wish your audience to remember. It should leave your audience with a sense of completeness. And if it is done well, it may even invite audience applause. A few of the devices that you may find useful are presented below.

Summary. When you want the audience to recall the major points of your speech, a review of these points may be helpful. Adlai Stevenson closed a eulogy to Winston Churchill by bringing together all of the attributes of the man that he had praised in his speech:

> The great aristocrat, the beloved leader, the profound historian, the gifted painter, the supurb politician, the lord of language, the wit—yes, and the dedicated brick layer—behind all of them was the man of simple faith, steadfast in defeat, generous in victory, resigned in age, trusting in a loving providence and committing his achievements and his triumphs to a higher power.[34]

In your early speeches, your summaries may take on the appearance of a simple relisting of the major points. As your skills grow, you will find ways of drawing your ideas together in fresh and stimulating ways.

Quotation. Speakers often conclude their messages with quotations. When the essence of your thoughts has been adequately captured in the language of another, you may borrow that language to effectively conclude your own ideas. When the source of the quotation is one held in esteem by your audience, your synthesis is strengthened and verified. A college student seeking to enlist audience support for anti-air-pollution measures concluded his speech by noting:

> In the words of Professor Morris B. Jacobs, former director of the Department of Air Pollution Control, "It is now time to end this plague. Time to look beyond narrow vested interests, to awake from slumbering too long—and save ourselves. We had better act now. It will soon be too late." [35]

Appeal. A speech designed to move an audience to action will fall short of its goal if the speaker concludes the address on a low key. A final appeal to action can enlist the deep emotional commitment of an audience. Professor Robert V. Andelson concluded his commencement address at Union Academy by inviting the students to pursue their quest for good answers to hard questions on the university level. He observed:

> . . . if you have a thirst for humane knowledge, if you have learned here how to stretch your minds, and want to keep on stretching them—come to us. We need you and we want you. And when you come, be persevering. Remember that amid all the spoon-feeding and busy-working and rat-capping and hell-raising, amid the Cliff notes and the roll calls and the snap tests and the beer busts—amid and in spite of all these things, if you seek diligently enough, and study hard enough, and wait long enough, you may find a couple of professors who will inspire you, and four or five books which will open new vistas for you. And as these professors and these books force you to think, who knows? Who knows but what out of your thinking may arise constructive ways of dealing with the terrible and solemn issues which imperiously confront our nation and our world.[36]

Reference to introductory materials. A reference to materials or ideas that were used in the introduction to your speech can serve to give psychological unity to your speech. Mary Wayman, whose introductory illustration about Nancy and Joe was mentioned earlier, concluded her speech by noting:

> Now Nancy, 22, and Joe, 27, both from "nice" families, are married and have a son who, due to his parents' disease, was born blind.[37]

Similarly, President Kennedy, who introduced his speech by saying "Today, in the world of freedom, the proudest boast is "Ich bin ein Berliner,'" concluded his speech with the words:

> All free men, wherever they may live, are citizens of Berlin, and therefore, as a free man, I take pride in the words, *"Ich bin ein Berliner."* [38]

Statement of personal intentions. Earlier we noted that a speaker may conclude a speech by appealing to the audience for action. The speaker may also bring power to a speech by alluding to his or her own intentions in the light of the position taken in the speech. Dr. Pinson, a Professor of Christian Ethics, in responding to the "Playboy Philosophy," concluded his speech by pledging:

> Others may go hopping down the bunny trail, but I'll follow Him who said, "I am the way, the truth, and the life. Follow Me." [39]

The devices that have been presented in this section need not be used singly. Most speakers combine a number of these devices to leave the audience with a message to recall and a reason for recalling it.

EXERCISES

VERIFICATION

5. List the six functions commonly assigned to introductions.

   a.

   b.

   c.

   d.

   e.

   f.

VERIFICATION

6. Place a check mark by each statement that reflects a function commonly assigned to speech introductions. (Caution: when finished, you should have identified six functions.)
   a. _____ Tell a funny story.
   b. _____ Focus attention on the subject.
   c. _____ Apologize for unpreparedness.
   d. _____ Reveal your life story.
   e. _____ Tell audience what you're going to tell 'em.
   f. _____ Beat around the bush.
   g. _____ Define crucial terms.

h. _____ Start with "I'd like to. . . ."
i. _____ Clearly state your subject or purpose.
j. _____ Illustrate importance of subject.
k. _____ Insult the audience.
l. _____ Establish personal expertise.

VERIFICATION

7. Of the four responses that follow, circle that which best identifies the five concluding devices discussed in this chapter.

   a. anecdotes, quotations, startling statements, appeals, and summaries

   b. statement of personal intent, summaries, appeals, quotations, reference to introduction

   c. statement of subject or purpose, statement to enhance credibility, statement to focus attention, statement of importance, statement of partition

   d. reference to introduction, appeal, psychological ending, quotations, statement of personal intent

VERIFICATION

8. Identify each of the devices defined below:

   a. ____________________ reiterates main points of the speech.
   b. ____________________ uses a restatement of the central idea as expressed by a credible source.
   c. ____________________ urges involvement or action.
   d. ____________________ provides psychological closure by relating ending to beginning.
   e. ____________________ commits speaker to continued action.

UTILIZATION

9. Match each descriptive label below with the letter of the appropriate example in list B.

   List A

   a. statements to focus attention _____
   b. statements to enhance credibility _____
   c. statements of importance _____
   d. statements of subject or purpose _____
   e. statements of partition _____
   f. summaries _____

g. concluding quotation _____

h. concluding appeal _____

i. concluding reference to introduction _____

j. statement of personal intentions _____

k. statements providing background _____

List B

1. My remarks this afternoon have offered two paths that you may walk: the path of pessimism and despair, and the path of optimism and renewed hope.
2. Having taught in elementary and secondary schools and having taught both undergraduate and graduate college level courses, I have viewed American education from perspectives as diverse as the front stoop of the little red schoolhouse and the pinnacle of the ivory tower.
3. Come let us join in this common cause. Let the whole world know that free Americans working together can bring light and hope where once there was only darkness and despair.
4. So today I wish to paint a picture in your minds—a picture of the first American.
5. When I was a little boy, my mother used to tell me to clean my plate because a lot of little boys were starving in India. Well—today I'm fat, and a lot of little boys are still starving in India.
6. I know that you will do what conscience dictates—but I can do no less than give freely of my time, talents, and resources to ensure that the majesty of America's great redwoods are preserved for all the generations that will be.
7. You may be thinking that the social security system is just for old people, but it's as close to you as your next paycheck.
8. The thoughts that I have shared with you were captured by the poet who said:

    Better that you care
    Better that you share
    Than you build a temple tall
    Which time must surely fall.
9. The transition from child to adult is best examined in three stages: prepubescence, pubescence, and adolescence.
10. I began today with a tribute to nature's song, but unless man develops a conscience, her song may soon be stilled.
11. Before discussing contemporary American patriots, it is important to note that patriotism does not mean blind allegiance to country—"My

country right or wrong." Rather, patriotism means dedication to this nation's principles and a dynamic commitment to righting social wrongs.

UTILIZATION

10. Analyze the introduction and conclusion below. Identify all of the devices used in each sample.

Introduction

School Bus Careens Off Mountain Road—
Victims Rescued by Helicopter

This is only one of many headlines that have dotted the nation's newspapers as a result of a government program known as MAST—Military Assistance to Safety and Traffic. Having spent two years in Vietnam, I have first hand knowledge of the importance of such a program in saving lives. There can be no doubt that the most effective way to save lives is to provide patients with prompt, on-the-scene medical treatment and with rapid transportation to a facility where their needs may be met fully. Today, I wish to familiarize you with MAST—a federally funded program designed to meet these needs. What is MAST? How successful has it been? And why, after five years of operation, has it been terminated? [10]

Conclusion

I hope that MAST is now more than a mysterious acronym to you. You have learned of its nature; you have seen its successes; and you have witnessed its demise. In the absence of the MAST program, we are left with a nagging question: How many people will needlessly die because prompt medical service is unavailable? Think about it. You can be sure that I will.[41]

UTILIZATION

11. Prepare an introduction and conclusion for the following outline. Choose a title for the speech. Your introduction must contain: statements to focus attention, statements to enhance credibility, statements of importance, statements providing background, statements of subject or purpose, and statements of partition. Your conclusion must contain three of the five devices identified in this section (summaries, quotations, appeals, reference to introduction, statement of personal intent).

Subject: Pollution
Purpose: To inform the audience of the four major kinds of pollution in America.

I. Pollution of the air

- A. Automotive pollution
- B. Industrial pollution
- C. Residential pollution
  - 1. Consumption of fuel
  - 2. Unsupervised burning

II. Pollution of water resources
- A. Industrial pollution
- B. Agricultural pollution
- C. Pollution by government organizations

III. Noise pollution
- A. Corporation noise
- B. Civic noise
- C. Individual noise

IV. Aesthetic pollution
- A. Commercial pollution
- B. Architectural pollution

Refining the Speech Outline

The preceding sections presented basic information about ways of patterning ideas and introducing and concluding speeches. You have already learned a great deal. In this final section, we will consider four guidelines that you may use as you refine your outline of main and supporting ideas.

Learn to Visualize Your Speech

The main ideas (I, II, III) and the subordinate ideas (A, B, 1, 2,) should be properly labeled and indented:

I.
- A.
  - 1.
  - 2.
    - a.
    - b.
- B.

II.

Visualizing your speech in this manner will clarify the relationships between your ideas.

Make Sure That the Main Ideas Stand Out

It is very easy to lose the central thoughts of your speech if they are buried in excess verbiage. There are several ways to highlight the main ideas.

Complete sentences may be used. Complete sentences will help you phrase your ideas clearly and precisely. Saying "Liberals are the cause of the nation's evils" instead of "Liberals cause evils" helps set the boundaries of your ideas.

Vivid language can sharpen otherwise dull images. Instead of saying "The children of migrant farm-workers lack educational opportunities," say "migrant farm-children are the learning poor."

You may phrase main ideas in parallel form. Parallel phrasing suggests to the audience that the ideas so expressed are of similar weight or importance. Consider the following example:

I. Civil disobedience subverts legal procedures for change.
II. Civil disobedience allows optional conformity to the law.
III. Civil disobedience stresses ends over means.

Each main idea should be distinguishable as a single idea. Instead of including two concepts in the same sentence ("Abortion is illegal and immoral") it is helpful to break the thoughts into separate units ("Abortion is immoral; abortion is illegal"). Also, avoid combining main ideas and supporting ideas in the same sentence. The statement, "The post office should be dismantled because its officials are corrupt and its operation is inefficient," should be arranged:

I. The post office should be dismantled.
  A. The officers are corrupt.
  B. The operation is inefficient.

The main ideas should stand as separate, distinct ideas. One main heading should not be capable of being subordinated under another heading. Consider this example:

I. The right to an abortion can be questioned.
II. Abortion is illegal.
III. Abortion is immoral.

Main headings II and III should fall directly under I:

I. The right to an abortion can be questioned.
   A. Abortion is illegal.
   B. Abortion is immoral.

Make Sure that the Supporting or Subordinate Ideas Contribute to the Coherence of the Speech

As with main points, subordinate points should be phrased as economically and vividly as possible. They also should be distinguishable as single ideas and should not be as important as the main ideas they are meant to support. Consider this example:

I. The pesticide Zoro is harmful to household pets.
   A. Dogs exposed to Zoro suffer loss of body hair.
   B. Other animals also are adversely affected by Zoro.
   C. Zoro also may be harmful to humans.

Subordinate statement B is ambiguous. Does it refer to household pets alone? Subordinate statement C is a different concept altogether and needs to be raised to the level of I. A better pattern of arrangement follows:

I. The pesticide Zoro is harmful to household pets.
   A. Dogs exposed to Zoro suffer loss of body hair.
   B. Cats exposed to Zoro are seized by hiccups.
II. The pesticide Zoro may also be harmful to humans.

When ordering subordinate points, or when ordering main ideas, the same pattern of organization should be used consistently at each level. However, different patterns may be used at different levels. Thus, I, II, and III may be topical; points A, B, and C under I may be chronological; and 1, 2, and 3 under I. A. may be spatial.

Use Transitions to Signal Movements from Point to Point

Transitions should effectively illustrate movement from introduction to body to conclusion, and from idea to idea within the body. Lively introductions and dramatic conclusions are important, but their impact will be lessened if the audience gets lost between ideas. There are several devices that provide "sign-posts" for the audience.

Signal words. There are any number of words and phrases that may indicate movement from idea to idea. For example:

"Next, we must consider . . . ."
"It follows that . . . ."
"The final stage is . . . ."

Numbers are also helpful:

"First, we must . . . ."
"Second, we can . . . ."
"My third point is . . . ."

Linking phrases. Linking phrases are useful in tying ideas together. Such phrases remind the audience of previous points as it previews the points to follow:

"More critical than . . . . is the question of . . . ."
"Not only has inflation led to . . . , but it has led to . . . as well."
"Now that the problem is clear, let us begin to examine the solution."

Rhetorical questions. These are stylistic devices that help your audience to anticipate changes in the direction of the speech.

"Where do we go from here?"
"Why does this problem continue to plague us?"
"What else can we expect?"

Your own common sense probably is the best judge of which transitional statements will work. Avoid, at all costs, the pretentiousness of the debater who, in loving form for its own sake, announces, "My third subpoint of analysis under my second contention is. . . ." Transitions should help the audience, not confuse them.

EXERCISES

VERIFICATION

12. List the four guidelines for refining the speech outline in the order in which they were presented.

 a.

 b.

 c.

 d.

VERIFICATION

13. Select from the following statements those that approximate each of the four guidelines (use a. b. c. d. designations above). (Caution: two distractors are included.)

a. _____ Central ideas emerge with clarity.

b. _____ Progressions of ideas are carefully signalled.

c. _____ Both reviews and previews major points.

d. _____ Ideas are reflected in schematic form.

e. _____ Orders ideas by increasing strength to effect psychological climax.

f. _____ Subordinate ideas reinforce the integrity of the central points.

UTILIZATION

14. The following statements are from an outline that has been scrambled. Reorganize these statements in proper order. Three of the statements belong in the introduction and two in the conclusion. The remainder of the statements belong in the body of the speech. As you order subpoints under main ideas in the body of the speech, consider the sequence that would seem most natural to an American audience.

What are these four miracles of contemporary American suburban architecture?

The crackerbox reborn lives on as the contemporary American "Ranch."

The lower level of the raised ranch, which peers out of half windows at the ground which hugs its waist, is normally used for play and work.

As a student of architecture, I have noted that suburbia has changed: your home is now reproduced not next door, but four whole gloriously different doors away.

The ranch home has three bedrooms.

In the years following World War II, the emerging suburbs of America consisted of tidy rows of cracker-box houses that differed only in the brick-a-brack that adorned them.

The middle level of the "tri" is for LDK.

The first level of the two story house is LDK and half bath.

The ranch home has a small living room, dining room, and kitchen.

The raised ranch is a ranch house standing tall.

The tri-level home is a smug compromise.

Ah, suburbia! How diverse thou art—the ranch, the raised ranch, the two story, and the tri-level.

The two-level house looks down condescendingly at its shorter neighbors.

The ranch home has one bathroom and, of course, an attached garage.

The top level of the two-story house is reserved for BR's and bath.

You've come a long way baby—or have you?

The lower level of the "tri" is for play.

The upper level of the raised ranch is simply the ranch raised.

The upper level of the "tri" is the BR's and bath.

UTILIZATION

15. There are two structural flaws in the outline that follows. Identify them.

Subject: Writing Skills

Purpose: To convince the audience that student writing skills are impoverished

I. National testing centers report declining scores
   A. College Entrance Examination Board (CEEB) scores of verbal aptitude show a consistent decline during the past five years.
      1. Five years ago the mean score was....
      2. Four years ago the mean score was....
      3. Three years ago the mean score was....
      4. Two years ago the mean score was....
      5. Last year the mean score was....

(Transition: further verification is provided by another prestigious assessment agency).

   B. The National Assessment of Educational Progress (NAEP) reports a decline.
      1. Elementary school students scored lower than when last tested, seven years ago.
      2. Secondary school students scored lower than when last tested seven years ago.
      3. Students had difficulty in both syntax and grammar.

(Transition: thus, major assessment agencies suggest that writing skills are declining. Further verification is provided by representatives of our nation's colleges and universities).

II. Colleges and universities report an increased need for remedial writing instruction.
   A. A large percentage of college freshmen fail writing competency tests and try to avoid courses which require the writing of term papers.
      1. At Midwestern University 25 percent of the freshmen fail the basic writing competency test.
      2. The Consortium of Eastern Colleges reports that 30 percent of their incoming freshmen fail the author's proficiency examination.

(Transition: but what do college instructors say about their students?)

   B. College instructors report that their students are impoverished in writing skills.
      1. In a recent survey of university professors, 60 percent of those sampled indicated that the majority of their students were "less than adequate" in composition.
      2. The National Association of Community College Instructors recently listed composition skills as the major weakness of community college students.

UTILIZATION

16. Choose a subject and a purpose that may be adequately developed using the following outline of main points and subordinate points. Your outline must satisfy the guidelines presented in the final section of this chapter.

I.

A.

1.

2.

(Transition)

B.

1.

2.

3.

(Transition)

II.

A.

1.

2.

3.

(Transition)

B.

Notes

1. Franklin D. Roosevelt, "Declaration of War," in Houston Peterson, *A Treasury of the World's Great Speeches* (New York: Simon and Schuster, 1954), p. 791.

2. Dean Brasser, Unpublished Manuscript, University of Wisconsin, 1972.

3. Dianne Klemme, "The Age of Gerontion," *Winning Orations* (1970):27–30.

4. Anthony F. Arpaia, "A Matter of Necessity," in Wil Linkugel, R. R. Allen, and Richard Johannesen, *Contemporary American Speeches,* (Belmont, Cal.: Wadsworth Publishing Co., 1965), pp. 240–50.

5. Charles Schaillol, "The Strangler," in Linkugel et al., *American Speeches,* 3d ed., pp. 260–64.

6. Martin Luther King, Jr., "Love, Law, and Civil Disobedience," in Linkugel, et al., *American Speeches,* 3d ed., pp. 62–81.

7. Phyllis Jones Springen, "The Dimensions of the Oppression of Women," *Vital Speeches* 37 (15 February 1970): 265–66.

8. J. William Middendorf, "World Sea Power," *Vital Speeches* 31 (1 January 1975): 166–69.

9. Harvey C. Jacobs, "The Great Race," *Vital Speeches* 41 (15 January 1975): 203–4.

10. Ralph Zimmerman, "Mingled Blood," in Linkugel et al., *American Speeches,* 2d ed., p. 200.

11. Marie Ransley, "The Life and Death of Our Lakes," in Linkugel et al., *American Speeches,* 3d ed., p. 64.

12. Susan Flanagan, "Formal Censorship is Counter Productive," Unpublished Manuscript, University of Wisconsin-Madison, 1974.

13. Brent Simmons, "As Time Runs Out," *Winning Orations* (1969): 75.

14. Thomas Peters, "No Provision for Now," *Vital Speeches* 37 (15 November 1970): 75.

15. Daniel J. Flood, "Projected Surrender of U.S. Canal Zone," *Vital Speeches* 41 (1 August 1975): 635.

16. James N. Sites, "The Over Regulation of Private Enterprise," *Vital Speeches* 41 (1 July 1975): 565.

17. Mary Katherine Wayman, "The Unmentionable Diseases," in Linkugel et al., *American Speeches* 3d ed., p. 200.

18. Klemme, "Gerontion," *Winning Orations* (1970): 27.

19. Nancy Strom, "Plants Have Feelings," Unpublished Manuscript, University of Wisconsin-Madison, 1975.

20. Jean Dohrer, "Our Forgotten Man," in Linkugel, *American Speeches,* 3d ed., p. 270.

21. Aristotle, *Rhetoric,* trans. Rhys Roberts (New York: Modern Library, 1954), p. 25.

22. Ralph Zimmerman, "Mingled Blood," in Linkugel et al., *American Speeches,* p. 200.

23. James N. Rowe, "An American Prisoner of War in South Vietnam," in Linkugel, *American Speeches* (1972), p. 46.

24. Felipe Ponce, "La Causa," in Linkugel et al., *American Speeches,* 3d ed., p. 67.

25. Henry Grady, "The New South," in A. Craig Baird, ed., *American Public Addresses 1740–1952* (New York: McGraw-Hill, 1956), p. 181.

26. Spiro Agnew, "Television News Coverage," in Linkugel et al., *American Speeches,* 3d ed., p. 192.

27. Springen, "Oppression," *Vital Speeches* 37: 265.

28. King, "Love, Law," in Linkugel et al. *American Speeches,* p. 71.

29. Rowe, "Prisoner of War," in Linkugel, et al., *American Speeches,* 3d ed., pp. 46–7.

30. H. Bell, "Does the Small Private College Have a Future?" *Vital Speeches,* 41, no. 7 (15 March 1975): p. 351.

31. Charles Cox, "The Insurance Industry," *Vital Speeches* 41, no. 7 (15 January 1975): p. 208.

32. Donald W. Whitehead, "Waiting the Judgment Day," *Vital Speeches* 41, no. 19, (15 July 1975): 595.

33. William G. Carleton, "Effective Speech in a Democracy," in Carroll C. Arnold, Douglas Ehninger, and John C. Gerber, *The Speaker's Resource Book,* 2d ed. (Chicago: Scott Foresman and Company, 1966), p. 7.

34. Stevenson, "Churchill," *Washington Post,* 29 January 1965, p. A5.

35. Schaillol, "The Strangler," in Linkugel et al., *American Speeches,* 3d ed., p. 264.

36. Robert V. Andelson, "Campus Unrest: The Erosion of Excellence," *Vital Speeches* 36 (1 August 1970): 621.

37. Wayman, "Diseases," in Linkugel et al. *American Speeches,* 3d ed., p. 204.

38. John F. Kennedy, "Ich Bin Ein Berliner," in Linkugel et al., *American Speeches,* 3d ed., p. 296.

39. William M. Pinson, Jr., "The Playboy Philosophy—Con," in Linkugel et al., *American Speeches,* 3d ed., p. 184.

40. Rollin Rieder, Unpublished Manuscript, University of Wisconsin, 1976.

41. Ibid.

5

informative speaking

learning objectives

By the conclusion of this chapter you will be able to:

1. Identify eight types of topics that are appropriate for informative speeches.
2. Match the types of speech topics with their definitions.
3. Identify the types of topics addressed in sample speech titles.
4. Provide a topic you feel prepared to speak about for each of the eight topic categories.
5. Identify two means of limiting topics.
6. Match the means of limiting topics with their descriptions.
7. Rank-order topics by degree of specificity.
8. Analyze the accuracy of a sample-narrowing process.
9. Narrow a topic using visual partitioning.
10. Identify the three informative requirements of a topic.
11. Match each informative requirement with a description of that requirement.
12. Identify violations of informative requirements by type.
13. Analyze a sample outline using the three informative requirements.
14. Construct a sample outline that meets the three informative requirements.
15. Identify nine kinds of expository materials.
16. Match each expository device with a description of that device.
17. Identify sample expository devices by type.

Recall
Comprehension
Application
Analysis
Synthesis

18. Analyze the use of expository devices in a brief sample speech.

19. Create a one to two minute speech on an abstract concept utilizing at least three expository devices.

20. Analyze sample speeches using an informative speech evaluation form.

21. Prepare and deliver an informative speech that meets the requirements of the informative speech evaluation form.

> Because information can change society, and because the amount of information doubles every fifteen years, our culture, if it is to become enriched and improved by its information, needs speakers and writers to digest and assimiliate this information and present it with clarity. The development of intelligent informative speakers is necessary to the improvement of our society, especially in our time.[1]
>
> Otis M. Walter

In the headnote above, it is observed that our society needs intelligent speakers and writers to help us cope with the "information explosion." As a college student, you are facing a very personal kind of knowledge explosion that may lead you to conclude, "Let society worry about its own information explosion. I have enough to do just trying to cope with my own."

However, as you grow in knowledge, there is cause for you to seek a commensurate growth in your ability to communicate that knowledge. In your college life, the ability "to digest and assimilate . . . information and present it with clarity" is relevant to effective performance in most courses. Beyond the campus, the ability to communicate information is central to effective performance in many careers.

The primary purpose of informative speaking is to provide information that may be understood and retained by an audience. You have already learned many of the skills that will help you to present information effectively. The skills of delivery, language usage, and organization, which were considered in the preceding chapters, are all relevant to informative speaking. By building on these basic skills, this chapter will help you to sharpen the focus of your informative speech and to select expository devices that will give clarity and interest to your ideas.

Sharpening the Informative Focus

In this section, you will be invited to consider topics that you may select for informative speaking. You also will be encouraged to narrow your topics to manageable proportions and to analyze the informative requirements of your topics.

Selecting a Topic

In the real world, informative speakers often have their topics selected for them: the police officer who is asked to address a service club is told that members would like to hear about burglary-prevention techniques; the minister is asked by members of the Bible study group to provide contemporary insights regarding Revelation; the banker, asked to address the Investment Club, is informed that they wish a market appraisal; the automotive engineer, asked to address a driver training class, is given the topic, "Preventive Maintenance"; and the tax consultant is asked to identify the most frequently overlooked business tax exemptions for the Business Club. In the world of work, the topics of informative speeches are also largely predetermined: the architect is scheduled to explain a building plan to a building commission; the salesman is given forty minutes to present a new product line to potential buyers; a social worker is asked to report to the city council about the new halfway house for juvenile offenders; and a dietician schedules a meeting with public health officials to discuss dietary programs for the aged.

However, in the public communication class the topics for informative speeches are usually not provided. You are expected to select a topic from your repertoire of experiences and to make that topic relevant and meaningful for your peers.

In the paragraphs that follow, we will identify eight categories of speech topics that are appropriate for informative speeches. As you read these paragraphs, ask yourself, "Do I have any experience with, or knowledge of, any subjects suggested by these categories?" When you find yourself answering yes, write the topics down for later consideration.

People. From Babe Ruth to Sandy Koufax, from Sojourner Truth to Gloria Steinem, from Adolf Hitler to Mahatma Gandhi, people form our heritage. An informative speech can help an audience to understand the salient forces in a person's life, the major events that shaped or were shaped by a person, and the contributions of an individual to the larger social fabric.

Places. Monuments, craters, mountains, cities, parks, and lakes have all served as speech topics. Since everyone has lived somewhere, even students who have not traveled widely can shed light on man-made and natural phenomena that are included in this category. One student described a thirty-three mile bicycle trail near his home town so vividly that five of his classmates went home with him that weekend to ride it.

Things. Americans are preoccupied with the marvels of technology. The products of our industrialized society—computers, satellites, deodorants, and "pacemakers"—may all command the attention of audiences. But audiences also may be interested in such non-man-made things as sharks, tarantulas, mushrooms, and African violets. Central to the hobbies and interests of most college students are "things" that can provide the basis for interesting, informative speeches.

Events. The history of the world is chronicled in events—major battles, elections, and assassinations are of immense social significance. The Japanese attack on Pearl Harbor, the bombing of Hiroshima, The Freedom March, the assassinations of John F. Kennedy and Martin Luther King, Jr., and the Kent State killings are significant events in recent American history. All cry out to be explained and understood. As speakers may try to accurately recapture and ponder the meanings of single events, they also may describe collections of events that have social significance—funerals, weddings, tribal dances, tax audit conferences, and bar mitzvahs.

Processes. Process speeches seek to clarify the stages of development of a man-made or natural phenomenon. Among the areas discussed in process speeches that students have given are: eutrophication (the aging process in lakes); the process of scientific inquiry; the stages of regeneration; the nature of metamorphosis; the stages of sleep; the electoral process; the stages of Project Apollo; the process of nuclear-energy production; and "belly dancing." Your hobbies, your studies, and your work experiences will suggest additional processes that audiences may find interesting and significant.

Concepts. Unlike people, places, things, events, and processes, which tend to be quite concrete, concepts refer to general ideas, theories, or thoughts and tend to be more abstract. Among the concepts that speakers have sought to clarify in informative speeches are God, love, virtue, duty, honor, academic freedom, equality, nonviolent resistance, patriotism, democracy, optimism, courage, the "big bang" theory of the universe, linguistic competence, and sexism. Although concepts are often subject to various interpretations, they are among the most significant topics for informative speeches.

Problems. Our world is plagued by problems. Inflation, recession, unemployment, war, hunger, pollution, disease, child abuse, energy shortages, crime, and crabgrass are a few. Since the quality of individual and corporate life will be determined largely by our ability to understand and master such problems, informative speeches regarding problems are very important. Since not all problems are global, national, or even regional in nature, students will find conditions in their state, city, and campus that merit the serious consideration of their peers.

Plans and policies. In response to problems, plans and policies are designed to organize action. In a complex society, programs of action are also often complex. Informative speakers must clarify the important dimensions of plans, programs, policies, and other courses of action. Among the plans and policies that students have addressed are the Equal Rights Amendment, school bussing, revisions in the judicial process, the negative income tax, tax reform, the decriminalization of marijuana, and programs for penal reform. Although problems and solutions are also the subject of persuasive speeches, there are moments when the purpose is to describe accepted information regarding problems and policies.

We hope that the above discussion has helped you to identify a number of suitable topics for your informative speech. As you sift through these topics in search of your final choice, consider the following three questions: (1) does this topic reflect my major interests, special qualifications, and past experiences? (2) does this topic invite the attention and interest of my intended audience? and (3) does this topic have significance?

The third question may require special clarification. There are many socially important topics that deserve the attention of intelligent speakers and audiences. Until these topics have been exhausted, resist the temptation to talk about "how to make a pizza," "how to serve a tennis ball," and "how to ride a pogo stick." Also, since public communication is essentially a verbal act, resist the temptation to bring to class the artifacts of trivial topics—trombones, duck calls, pet snakes, and a Honda 750.

Limiting the Topic

Since class time is limited, most college public communication instructors favor the presentation of short speeches. You have probably learned that it is more difficult to prepare a short speech than it is to prepare a long one. Your major problem is the task of so limiting a topic that it may be treated with integrity in a four or five minute address. In this section, we will consider two solutions to this problem.

Focusing on crucial aspects. The first means of limiting a topic is to focus only on crucial aspects. This solution sacrifices depth of treatment for breadth of treatment. When an overview of a topic area is desired, this is the preferred system for limiting the topic.

Imagine, for example, that your instructor wishes to remind you of the major sources of information for speeches. Now this is a very broad topic, but since your instructor is convinced that you have previously received in-depth instruction in library research in high school, a brief survey of the major sources is adequate. How might such a speech be focused?

Purpose: To Remind the Class of the Major Sources of Speech Information

I. The speaker may consult human resources.
   A. Conversations with friends, family members, and teachers are often helpful.
   B. Formal interviews with subject matter experts are worthwhile.
   C. Polls can provide useful survey data.
   D. A letter to congressional representatives can secure important information.

II. The speaker may consult printed resources.
   A. Encyclopedias provide brief overviews.
   B. Articles in magazines and periodicals, which are indexed in *The Reader's Guide to Periodical Literature*, provide up to date, brief analyses.
   C. The publication, *Facts on File,* provides excellent reviews of current events.
   D. Books, indexed in the card catalog, offer extended, in-depth analyses.

While this outline does not provide for concrete information on using particular resources, it does provide a broad survey that may jog your memory.

Narrowing the topic. In addition to focusing on crucial aspects of a topic, speakers may limit topics by focusing on highly specific aspects of a broader topic area. Imagine, for example, that you have been given five minutes to talk to an eighth-grade class about sources of information for speeches. Since your audience members know very little about research, you feel that it is important to provide detailed information about a specific resource so that they begin to see the potentialities of individual sources. You would probably proceed with a narrowing process such as the process represented in figure 6.

Given that you finally choose *The New York Times* as the source of information you wish to consider, there is still much to be said in

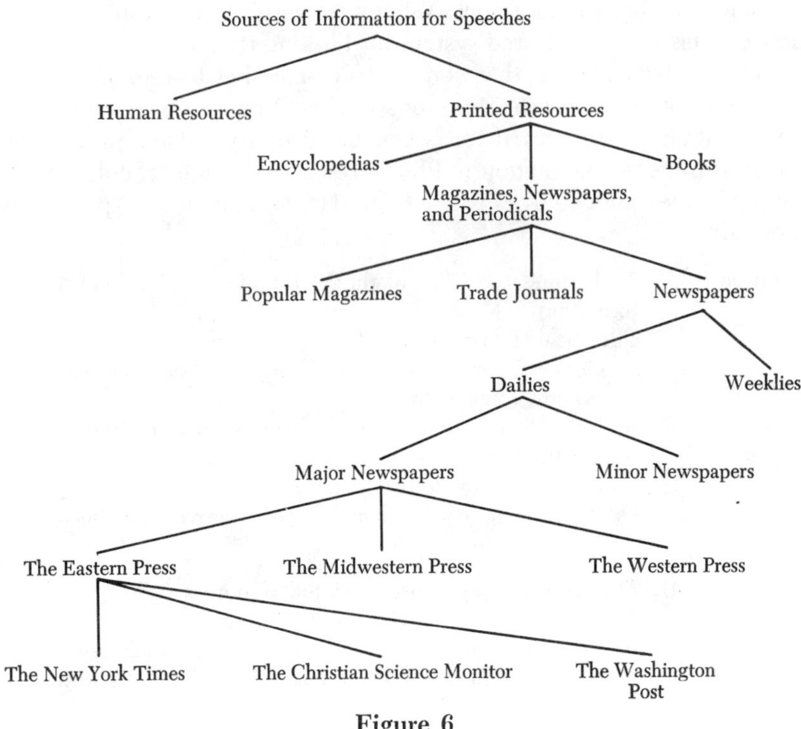

Figure 6

a five minute speech. You may describe the contents of the daily and Sunday editions; you may discuss the news reporting and editorial policies of the newspaper; you may discuss indexing procedures that might aid the student in research. Given five minutes, you may provide a detailed and informative account of a major source of available information.

Analyzing the Informative Requirements of a Topic

When seeking to inform an audience about a topic, it is important that your message be characterized by *accuracy*, *completeness*, and *unity*. To do less is to betray the informative intent. The importance of offering an accurate, complete, and unified view of subjects was explained by Wilson and Arnold in the following way:

> The speaker who undertakes to explain how a tape recorder works will err seriously if he alleges that all tape recorders use vacuum tubes for sound amplification (many use transistors); he will err in a different

> way if he neglects to discuss the playback systems most recorders have; and he will err in another fashion if he does not make it clear that the entire mechanical system exists to preserve and repeat sound . . . . His listeners may not reject him as a person for this error of fact, his omission, and his disregard for the total meaning of his material; but they will not understand tape recorders unless they understood them before. The speaker did not put into his discourse those things that must be there if talk is to inform or teach: accuracy, completeness, unity.[2]

As you prepare your speech, you must ensure that you meet the informative requirements of your subject.

To illustrate these informative requirements in action, let us imagine that you are a college zoology major and return to your old high school to visit your former zoology teacher. As you meet her in the hallway, she says, "Am I glad to see you. I have to run home and take my husband to the hospital. Will you take my class? You can handle it—they are just dissecting frogs today." Recalling chapter 4 of your public communication textbook, you mentally organize your ideas as you walk to the zoology classroom. Your basic plan looks something like this:

Purpose: To Inform the Audience about the Process of Dissecting a Frog

I. It is important to prepare carefully for the dissection.
   A. Get your utensils.
      1. You will need a dissecting pan.
      2. You will need a scalpel and scissors.
      3. You will need two probes and a tweezers.
      4. You will need dissecting pins.
   B. Wet a paper towel and place it over the dissecting pan.
   C. Place the frog on top of the paper towel.

(Transition: Now that you're ready (shudder), let's get on with it.)

II. The dissection process consists of four stages.
   A. You will begin by making three incisions with the scalpel.
      1. The first incision proceeds from the throat to the lower portion of the body on the ventral side.
      2. The second incision crosses the body just above the forelegs, forming a *T* with the vertical incision.
      3. The third incision crosses the lower body just above the hind legs, forming an *I* with the other incisions.
   B. You must then peel the skin and muscle away.
      1. The flaps of skin are opened like a single-serving cereal box with each of the two flaps opening from the center.

2. As each flap is opened, the scalpel is used to cut away binding muscle tissue.
3. Pin the skin flaps to the wax in the dissecting pan with the dissecting pins.

C. You must remove organs in layers (being careful not to damage adjacent organs) and identify them against the anatomy chart.
1. Remove the fat deposits, stomach, intestines, and liver.
2. Remove the gall bladder, spleen, and heart.
3. Remove the lungs and kidneys.

D. You may now observe the brain.
1. Scrape away the skull with the scalpel.
2. Remove the brain.

(Transition: The hard part is over, but don't forget to clean up the mess.)

III. The cleaning-up process has five steps.
A. Wrap frog remnants in the paper towel and place them in a plastic-lined waste basket.
B. Clean the dissecting pan with detergent and water, and put it away.
C. Clean the utensils and put them away.
D. Clean the table and working area.
E. Wash your hands.

(Transition: It's all over, but what have you learned?)

IV. The dissection of a frog provides the following crucial insights.
A. The individual organs of a frog closely resemble miniature versions of those of humans.
B. The interrelation of organs in a frog reminds the student of the dynamic interrelationships of organs in humans.

You have met the informative requirements of your subject. Your description of the process accurately portrayed the steps in the process. Your description covered all of the stages. Furthermore, you ensured that your presentation had unity by identifying the crucial insights that the students acquired.

As you approach each topic, engage in the same sort of analysis to ensure that your treatment has integrity. Once you have structured a sound outline, characterized by accuracy, completeness, and unity, you need only to search for expository materials that will provide elaboration for your outline and make your ideas clear and interesting. In the next section, we will consider the common types of expository materials that speakers have found useful.

EXERCISES

VERIFICATION

1. Identify the eight types of topics presented in the textbook.

VERIFICATION

2. Match the names in 1, above, with the following definitions. (Caution: one of the definitions does not apply.)
   a. ____________________ products of a technological society
   b. ____________________ abstract ideas
   c. ____________________ happenings
   d. ____________________ individuals or groups
   e. ____________________ social needs
   f. ____________________ solutions
   g. ____________________ cities, lakes, and trails
   h. ____________________ concrete ideas
   i. ____________________ stages or sequences

UTILIZATION

3. Next to each speech title listed below, write the topic category represented.
   a. ____________________ The Wonders of Bryce Canyon
   b. ____________________ The Christian Life
   c. ____________________ Nixon: the Man and the Myth
   d. ____________________ The Gemini Capsule: A Home Away from Home
   e. ____________________ The Causes of Teacher Strikes

f. ______________________ 7 December 1941: The Day that Will Live in Infamy

g. ______________________ The Kennedy-Griffin Bill: A Response to Our Health Care Crisis

h. ______________________ You Can Be Bigger than Life: Enlarging Color Photographs

UTILIZATION

4. For each of the topic categories listed above, provide a specific subject you feel prepared to speak about. Share ideas from each category with the class.

VERIFICATION

5. List the two means of limiting a topic.

VERIFICATION

6. Match the names in five above with the following descriptions. (Caution: one of the descriptions does not apply.)

a. ______________________ Highlighting significant aspects

b. ______________________ Clustering topics

c. ______________________ Limiting scope to a specific part of the subject

UTILIZATION

7. Examine the statements presented below. Rank-order the statements, with the most specific receiving a rank of 1, the least specific a rank of 5.

a. _____ Tribal Leadership among the Apaches

b. _____ Cochise: Chief and Warrier

c. _____ Native American Indians

d. _____ The Apache Tribe

e. _____ Indians of the Southwest

UTILIZATION

8. Analyze the sample of a narrowing process in figure 7. Underline any item or items that break the natural flow from general to specific.

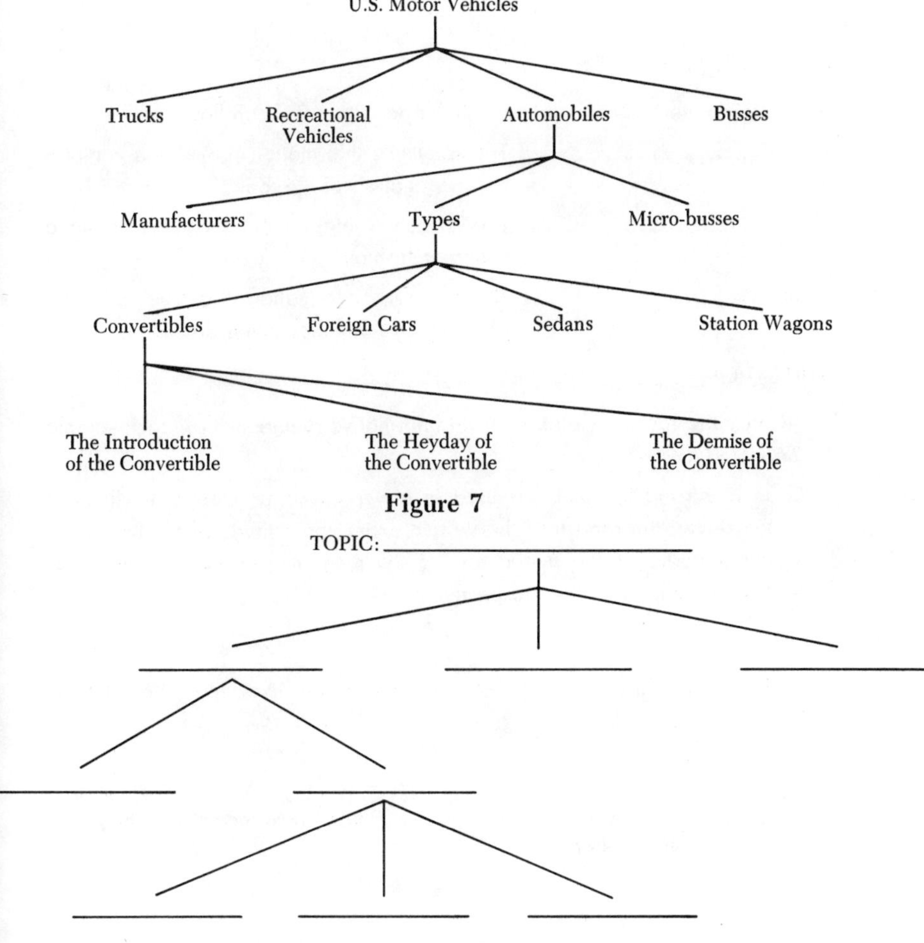

Figure 7

Figure 8

UTILIZATION

9. Using the graph in figure 8, select and narrow a topic of your choice. The topic must illustrate the substructure indicated by the graphic partitions.

VERIFICATION

10. Identify the three informative requirements of a topic.

VERIFICATION

11. Match the names in 10 above with the descriptions that follow.

    a. ____________________ The speaker's information provides a comprehensive analysis of the topic.

    b. ____________________ The speaker's information is constructed in a coherent fashion.

    c. ____________________ The speaker's information is a true reflection of the events or ideas being discussed.

UTILIZATION

12. Identify the specific violation of an informative requirement in each sample presented below.

    a. In discussing the methods used in driver education classes, I will treat the driver, the road test, the written exam, the attitude of the instructor, the attitudes of the public toward the program, the cost of the class, and the attitude of the prospective driver.

    b. There are three branches of government: the executive, the military, and the judicial.

    c. In most states in this country, the branches of government are the township, the city, and the state.

UTILIZATION

13. Analyze the following sample outline with respect to its fulfillment of the three informative requirements (accuracy, completeness, and unity).

Topic: The Eating Habits of Americans
Body:

I. Most American families eat three meals a day.
   A. Breakfast is usually eaten anytime between daybreak and the beginning of work or school.
   B. Lunch is served traditionally at noon.
   C. Dinner is served between five and seven o'clock in the evening.

II. The food habits of most American families are relatively standardized.
   A. Breakfast consists of a beverage and cereal, or bacon eggs, and toast, or simply toast or a sweet roll.
   B. Lunch usually consists of a sandwich with soup, potato chips, or french fries.
   C. Dinner is usually a full meal with meat, vegetable, potatoes, and dessert.

UTILIZATION

14. On a separate piece of paper, construct a sample outline that satisfies the three requirements for an informative speech (presented in this chapter), and the guidelines for a speech outline (presented in chapter 4).

Selecting Expository Devices

Expository devices are used to give clarity and interest to the speaker's ideas. In this section, nine expository devices will be considered. As you read this section, seek to determine which of these devices will be especially useful in developing the topic that you have selected for your informative speech.

Definitions

A person who wishes to explain complex ideas must often provide definitions of those terms that may confuse the audience. Dictionaries and other reference works are valuable sources of simple explanations. However, conveying the dictionary definition of *homothallic as* "having only one haploid phase producing genetically compatible gametes" may only further confuse the audience. Definitions such as these are precise, but phrased in terms unfamiliar to most people.

Ronee Ross avoided this difficulty by using familiar terms to explain the "food stamp concept." She stated:

> Households which meet uniform eligibility standards with regard to income and economic resources may purchase each month a specified allotment of food coupons or stamps; the size of the allotment depends on family size, and the price paid depends on household income level.[3]

When dictionary definitions are too technical, speakers are well advised to define terms in more familiar words.

Also, personal experience may be used to convey the meaning of a term, especially one whose meaning is elusive or abstract. Major Nick Rowe, an American prisoner of war during the Vietnam conflict, illustrated the use of personal experience in defining the term *sacrifice:*

> When you see an American prisoner giving up his meager ration of fish, just so another American who is sick can have a little bit more to eat, that is sacrifice. Because . . . you have very little and you give it up, then you're hurting yourself, and that is true sacrifice.[4]

The purpose of a definition is to make the meaning of a word clear. When the dictionary definition just won't do, you are well advised to define the term in your own words or to offer a personal reference that conveys the meaning the term has for you.

Examples

One of the best ways to convey meaning is to use simple, concrete examples. There are two types of examples: *brief examples* and *extended examples*. Examples may be real events or they may be hypothetical. Invented examples should be believable and contain elements familiar to the audience.

In a speech on unemployment, a student used brief examples to clarify his point:

> Trends in unemployment have varied considerably since 1925. For example, in 1931, the height of the depression, 25% of the labor force was jobless. In contrast, 12 years later World War II put the unemployment rate at 1%.[5]

Brief examples clarify the speaker's idea with precision and economy.

William Banowsky, President of Pepperdine University, used an extended example to illustrate the merits of perseverance and determination:

> The story of America's greatest statesman is, likewise, not a story of early success, but one of dogged perseverance. He *failed* in business in 1831, was *defeated* for State Legislator in 1832, again *failed* in business in 1833, was *elected* to the State Legislature in 1834. His *sweetheart died* in 1836. He was *defeated* for Speaker in 1838, was *defeated* for Elector in 1840, and was *defeated* for Congress in 1843. Finally, he was *elected* for one term in Congress in 1846, only to be *defeated* again for Congress in 1848. He was *defeated* for the Senate in 1855, was *defeated* for Vice-President in 1856, and was *defeated* again for the Senate in 1858. Finally, in 1860, he was *elected* President of the United States. These were just a few rough spots in the life of Abraham Lincoln.[6]

An extended example may capture the essence of an idea in a dramatic and powerful way.

Hypothetical examples enable speakers to take an idea and present it in its most extreme or dramatic form. In her speech "What Is Totalitarianism?" Lauralee Peters dramatized the meaning of totalitarianism through the hypothetical example that follows:

> Perhaps the best description to date of the perfected totalitarian system is provided by George Orwell's novel, *1984*. Orwell describes for us a state which has assumed almost infinite power over the lives of its people. Two-way telescreens placed in all public and private places enable the state to observe and listen to the citizens at all times; the Ministry of Truth rewrites history to agree with the party line and, using the telescreen, invades the lives of the people constantly with official propaganda; and finally a state language, Newspeak, is adopted, whose vocabulary expresses only those concepts the state deems desirable. Here we see the ultimate end of the totalitarian state. The utilization of *all* possible means of control to establish the ultimate supremacy of the state in all aspects of the peoples' lives.[7]

Examples, brief or extended, real or hypothetical, are a powerful way of making ideas clear and interesting.

Statistics

Statistical or numerical data is a useful resource for explaining the scope or significance of a problem or the costs of a program. A speech on alcoholism, for instance, may use such data to indicate how many people are alcoholics, how many are being treated, what percentage are from a middle-class bracket. Felipe Ponce underscored the educational problems faced by Chicanos in this manner:

> Chicanos average 3.9 years less education than Anglo or white Americans—1.6 years less than blacks. In Texas, for example, 80 percent of Chicano students drop out before they graduate from high school.[8]

In this instance, the basic statistical data provided a crisp indication of the seriousness of the problem.

The challenge in using such information is to make it meaningful to the audience. Does the audience, or anyone, comprehend a $1.1 billion cost overrun in a building project? What does a $3 million cut in grants to vocational schools mean? Figures must be given meaning through an interpretation that is consonant with their impact and the reason for using them. Relating general statistical data to a specific situation can dramatize stale numbers and give the audience a heightened awareness of a problem. Patricia Hayes provided an excellent example of personalizing statistics in a speech on suicide:

> Dr. Dana Farnsworth, a leading expert in the field of mental health, lists some rather ominous nationwide statistics for colleges. He stresses that for each 10,000 students, 1,000 students will have emotional conflicts severe enough to warrant professional help, 300–400 will have feelings of depression deep enough to impair efficiency, 5–10 will attempt suicide, and 1–3 will succeed in taking his own life. If these statistics are true, my university should encounter 15–45 suicide attempts of which 3–5 will be successful.[9]

Since using exact figures (such as "148,392 babies were born in Two Dot over a 183 day period") can be cumbersome, round off such expressions: "About 150,000 babies were born in Two Dot over a six month period." You might add the following elaboration: "That translates to 25,000 per month, 833 per day, 35 per hour, or about 1 every two minutes."

Quotations

Instead of relying solely on your own inventive powers, you may use other people's words to clarify ideas. Quotations may serve to define, clarify, or otherwise convey a message in terms more precise than those you could create on your own. When the source of the quoted material is a well-known source, quotations may also give added credibility to your message.

Dianne Klemme, in describing the "limbo" in which the aged find themselves, used T. S. Eliot's poem, "Gerontion" to clarify the life of the aged in America:

Here I am, an old man in a dry month,
Being read to by a boy, waiting for rain . . .
I have lost my sight, smell, hearing, taste and touch,
How should I use them for your closer contact? [10]

Nancy Strom used quoted material to amplify her discussion of experimental research on the "feelings" of plants:

> The staff of the Chicago Tribune devised an experiment to investigate whether talking to plants made any difference . . . The results were that, "Those verbally stroked with tender loving care became perk and through a sophisticated plant language the staff began suggesting story ideas to all the editors. Those plants which had been ignored sulked, shriveled up, turned yellow around their edges and dropped their leaves. Those cursed out turned mushy, became comatose, and perished." [11]

As a final example, Henry Kissinger turned to the eminent British statesman, Winston Churchill, for a comment on the state of the world:

> A half-century ago Winston Churchill, in his book *The World Crisis,* observed that in happier times it was the custom for statesmen to "rejoice in that protecting Providence which had preserved us through so many dangers and brought us at last into a secure and prosperous age." But "little did they know," Churchill wrote, "that the worst perils had still to be encountered, and the greatest triumphs had yet to be won." [12]

Whether your source is a poet, a sage, or the grocer down the street, drawing on his or her expertise may assist in communicating your ideas in a clear and lively manner.

Visual Materials

The use of visual materials may enhance your attempt to convey information. Adlai Stevenson's use of photographs to demonstrate the existence of Russian missiles on Cuban soil is a dramatic example of the effect visual aids may have. A portion of Stevenson's address before the United Nations Security Council is reprinted below.

> I doubt if anyone in this room, except possibly the representative of the Soviet Union, has any doubt about the facts. But in view of his statements and the statements of the Soviet Government up until last Thursday, when Mr. Gromyko denied the existence or any intention of installing such weapons in Cuba, I am going to make a portion of the evidence available right now. If you will indulge me for a moment, we will set up an easel here in the back of the room where I hope it will be visible to everyone.

[Enlargements of aerial photographs were then placed on display, one by one, in the Security Council chamber.] .

The first of these exhibits shows an area north of the village of Candelaria, near San Cristóbal, southwest of Havana. A map, together with a small photograph, shows precisely where the area is in Cuba.

The first photograph shows the area in late August, 1962; it was then, if you can see from where you are sitting, only a peaceful countryside (figure 9).

The second photograph shows the same area one day last week. A few tents and vehicles had come into the area, new spur roads had appeared, and the main road had been improved (figure 10).

The third photograph, taken only twenty-four hours later, shows facilities for a medium-range missile battalion installed. There are tents for four or five hundred men. At the end of the new spur road there are seven one-thousand-mile missile trailers. There are four launcher-erector mechanisms for placing these missiles in erect firing position. This missile is a mobile weapon, which can be moved rapidly from one place to another. It is identical with the thousand-mile missiles which have been displayed in Moscow parades (figure 11).

All of this, I remind you, took place in twenty-four hours.[13]

A speaker may use slides, movies, diagrams, maps, graphs, models, or the object itself in aiding audience understanding. The use of these aids, or others that might be available, is limited by several factors. First, is there sufficient time to set up equipment, such as projectors, to use in displaying aids? If not, then presenting the material in other forms may be more appropriate. Second, are you able to use the equipment? This may seem obvious, but too many speakers have been embarrassed by their own fumbling with movie reels, with tape machines, or with the removal of slides that, when shown, were upside down and backwards. Careful preparation of the materials will eliminate these problems.

Visual aids may be useful when they are relevant to the subject, can be seen easily by the audience, and can be operated or handled smoothly and without undue disruption. Talk to the audience rather than to the aid; control audience attention by directing them to each item or object you wish to illustrate; and use projections of pictures rather than passing out items. Finally, let the aids supplement your speech, rather than supplant it. The audience should not be so entranced or confused by the aid that their attention is drawn from the message to the aid itself.

Figure 9

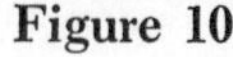

Figure 10

Figure 11

Comparisons and Contrasts

An audience can be led from what is known and familiar to an understanding of the unknown or unfamiliar through the use of comparisons or contrasts. A complex nuclear reaction can be explained by comparing it to the action on a pool table when the cue ball strikes the lead ball during the "break." Or the meaning of an "informed electorate" may be made clear by contrasting it with the voting behavior of an uninformed voter.

Joseph Palmer used both *contrast* and *comparison* techniques in discussing the varying approaches of African leaders to their problems:

> It is fascinating to observe the diversity of approaches of political leaders to this dialogue with constituencies. The intonation may be

> that of Oxford, the Sorbonne, or of a midwestern American university. The symbols may be capitalistic, Marxian, or traditional. The techniques may be democratic, authoritarian, tribal, or a blend of all three.
>
> In every case, the Africans are busy adapting a variety of local equivalents, based on their own experience and psychological outlook. Thus, the roasted whole sheep may substitute for the cold-chicken political supper, the shade tree for the town hall, and the cock or crested crane for the donkey or the elephant.[14]

In the first paragraph, Palmer presented contrasting options available to the leaders; in the second paragraph, he used comparisons to depict political symbols that dominate the African experience.

Greg Cairns offered another example of comparison in a speech entitled, "Sneaking Sissyism":

> You all know what a sissy is. He was that neighborhood panty-waist who was too chicken to take a dare. If you called him names, he would not fight you. Instead, he would run home to Momma. If the gang crossed the creek by means of a log, he would take the bridge. The sissy in the group was the kid who always *took the easy way out.*
>
> I believe that too many of American youth are acting like sissies. Too many of us always take the easy way out.[15]

After defining "sissy" in familiar terms, Cairns extended this term to American youth in general. The value of his comparison lies in the similarities perceived between a sissy who takes the easy way out of difficulties and the actions of contemporary American youth.

Repetitions

This device brings ideas to the forefront in a clear, and often dramatic, fashion. A student offered this analysis of the death of a great conductor:

> The January 17 issue of the New York Times carried the headline, "Arturo Toscanini is dead." Newspaper boys shouted from the street corners of Milan, "The Maestro is dead." The NBC Radio Symphony in Radio City gave a concert in his honor . . . The Maestro is dead. La Scala in Milan was closed down, and a special mass was said in St. Peter's . . . the Maestro is dead.[16]

The repetition of "the Maestro is dead" brought together unique events and unified them by reference to a single dramatic phrase. Particularly effective in persuasive settings, as in Martin Luther King, Jr.'s repetitive use of the phrase "I have a dream," the device also can help to get across the principal item of knowledge in an informative speech.

Descriptions

Similar to the example, this device often portrays the physical characteristics of an object or environment. When constructed in vivid language, the description imparts a sense of having been there. The speaker creates a "word picture" that visualizes the situation in a clear and dramatic manner. Nancy Frank, in speaking of prisons, used the following description:

> Waupun is a maximum security prison. We were searched for metal before entering the building. The guards wore uniforms that made them look like policemen. The cells were small with a bunk suspended from the wall by two thick chains. There were no windows in the cell. And where there should have been a fourth wall there was only the barred door that closes every night before the warden, the cooks, the librarian, and the psychologist go home. It especially struck me that in Waupun no one smiled.[17]

A more detailed narrative is Robert J. Havighurst's exposition on the American family. Havighurst described the "typical" home at the turn of the century:

> What was the home like fifty years ago? There was the parlor, always cold and clean and quiet, with an organ which was pumped with the feet, a hard horsehair sofa, and a photograph album. The sitting room was more cheerful, with its baseburner standing in the middle of the room on a metal sheet to protect the carpet, the coals glowing red-hot through the isinglass windows of the stove, the stove pipe going straight up through the ceiling to lend a little warmth to the bedroom above; the coal scuttle beside the stove, half full of coal, and garnished with nutshells and apple cores. On the library table a big kerosene lamp shedding a yellow glow, and the latest copies of *Harper's Bazaar* and *Youth's Companion*. Beside the table a big rocking chair, in which mother rocked the baby to sleep, singing lullabies. And I almost forgot to mention the brick sewn up in a piece of carpet, and used as a door-stop.
>
> In the kitchen there was the range, with a fire burning briskly, and the oven door open to warm the room on a cold morning, while oatmeal cooked in the double boiler and eggs and bacon sizzled in the frying pan. At the sink was the cistern pump for rain water, and beside it stood the pail of drinking water, with a long-handled dipper. Down in the cellar was the vegetable room with a bin of potatoes and a sack of turnips and a barrel of apples.
>
> Let us not omit from this picture the icy-cold bedroom, with the wash-water frozen in the washbowl on the washstand on winter morn-

> ings; the Saturday-night bath ritual in the washtub in the kitchen; the souring milk and the running butter during hot summer days, and the dread of typhoid fever always threatening to break into epidemic proportions.[18]

Do you feel like you've been there? Description can make unknown places vivid and concrete.

Restatements

Expressing an idea in more than one way may be a valuable aid in getting your meaning across. You prepare your audience for this device with expressions such as "putting it another way . . ." or "in other words . . ." Johnstone Patrick clarified the nature of power in the following excerpt from his speech on "The Problem of Power":

> So many who so often misquote a certain celebrated passage from a letter Lord Acton sent to Bishop Mandell Creighton, in 1887, stop short of what he really said. Acton actually said, "Power tends to corrupt, and absolute power corrupts absolutely. Great men are almost always bad men, even when they exercise influence and not authority: still more when you superadd the tendency or the certainty of corruption by authority . . ." Acton did not mean that St. Paul and Dante and Shakespeare were either great or were bad. He was thinking of men like Julius Caesar and Frederich the Great and Napoleon. Shelley expresses the same conviction more explosively and more poetically:
>
> Power like a desolating pestilence,
> Pollutes whate'er it touches; . . .
>
> Shelley was an anarchist; Acton a Victorian Liberal. Both, for all they were worth, detested dictators.[19]

In this example, Patrick used two different quotations to state and then restate the central idea he wished to develop.

You might wish to use a narrative form for restating your point. Martin Luther King, Jr. used this approach in elaborating on his assertion that "the end represents the means in process and the ideal in the making":

> In other words, we cannot believe, or we cannot go with the idea that the end justifies the means because the end is pre-existent in the means. So the idea of non-violent resistance, the philosophy of non-violent resistance, is the philosophy which says that the means must be pure as the end, that in the long run of history, immoral destructive means cannot bring about moral and constructive ends.[20]

Whatever the subject, a restatement of the idea in other words helps capture its essential meaning and gives the audience a better chance to understand its nature or its significance.

EXERCISES

VERIFICATION

15. Identify the nine kinds of expository devices.

VERIFICATION

16. Match the kinds of expository devices with the descriptions that follow. (Caution: two of the definitions do not apply.)

a. ______________ may be real or hypothetical.
b. ______________ can lend added credibility to your message if the source is respected.
c. ______________ emphasizes similarities or dissimilarities.
d. ______________ should be rounded off and interpreted.
e. ______________ is a simple declaration.
f. ______________ those that are too technical should be avoided.
g. ______________ should supplement your speech, not replace it.
h. ______________ appeals to audience prejudice.
i. ______________ means "to put it another way"
j. ______________ means "to put it the same way"
k. ______________ can provide a sense of having been there.

UTILIZATION

17. Identify each of the following sample expository devices, by type:

a. ______________ The hallway was long, dark, and narrow. Unshaded light bulbs, hung at long intervals, cast eerie shadows against the rough hewn walls.

b. ______________________ A megalomaniac is the sort of person who believes that if the universe ever has a central ruler, she'll be it.

c. ______________________ Representative of this type of mountain are Mt. Fuji in Japan and Mt. Kilimanjaro in Africa.

d. ______________________ The essence of this thought was captured so eloquently by Dr. Dudley Walmsby when he said, "Sexism will cease when men have babies."

e. ______________________ The helix  a slinky-like visual symbol, can be used to visualize the growth of communication skills in the child.

f. ______________________ He brought joy, but he could not stay. He brought hope, but he could not stay. He brought peace, but he could not stay.

g. ______________________ The mean score of college freshmen on the manual dexterity test was 4.2 on a 10 point scale. You may interpret that as you wish, but I would advise most of you to avoid a career in chicken plucking.

h. ______________________ Which is to say, where argument fails, ignorance prevails.

i. ______________________ How unlike the American concept of freedom of the press is that of the Chinese. In Peking the party rules the press; in Washington the press criticizes the party. In Peking the press reports events; in Washington the press helps shape events.

UTILIZATION

18. Analyze the minispeech that follows, and identify the main expository devices used in each paragraph.

The Elusive Nature of Love

Many who have tried to understand the nature of love have concluded in despair that it is impossible to specify in advance who will inspire love, under what conditions, or why. They have resonated to Durrell's poetic definition of love:

> It may be defined as a cancerous growth of unknown origin which may take up its site anywhere without the subject knowing or wishing it. How often have you tried to love the "right" person in vain even when your heart knows it has found him after so much seeking? No, an eyelash, a perfume, a haunting walk, a strawberry on the neck, the smell of almonds on the breath—these are the accomplices the spirit seeks out to plan your overthrow.

Other writers have tried to explicate *facets* of romantic love. Delightful essays have been written, for example, by Reik (1943); Beigel (1951); Maslow (1954); Fromm (1956); Goode (1959); and Hunt (1959). These analysts have often provided compelling—but unnervingly inconsistent—insights into the nature of passionate love.

Contradictions also are found in the voluminous folk sayings addressed to the topic of love. The person who is concerned with predicting the effect of separation upon his romance, for example, will find that folk wisdom has a good deal to say, much of it contradictory: "Out of sight out of mind"; "Absence makes the heart grow fonder"; "Absence lessens half-hearted passions, and increases great ones."

Disagreements such as these led Finck (1891) to the conclusion that "Love is such a tissue of paradoxes, and exists in such an endless variety of forms and shades, that you may say almost anything about it that you please, and it is likely to be correct.[21]

UTILIZATION

19. Create a one to two minute minispeech on an abstract concept, using at least three different kinds of expository devices. Underline each expository device used, and label each device in the margin. Among the abstract concepts that you may amplify, are the following:

truth	friendship	loyalty
justice	freedom	joy

mercy	patriotism	duty
love	dedication	faith

Preparing Your Informative Speech

In this chapter, and in chapters preceding this one, you have acquired all of the competencies needed for preparing and delivering an informative speech. In this section, we will first present a sample informative speech evaluation form that identifies relevant categories. We will then conclude with sample speeches that you will be asked to analyze.

Informative Speech Evaluation Form

Introduction *Comments*

Statement to Focus Attention
Statement to Enhance Credibility
Statement of Importance
Statement Providing Background
Statement of Subject or Purpose
Statement of Partition

Body

Major Points
1.
2.
3.
Clarity of Subpoints
Types of Expository Devices Used
1.
2.
3.
Use of Transitions Within the Body

Conclusion

Devices Used
1.
2.
3.
Effectiveness

Language Usage

Appropriateness
Clarity
Vividness

Delivery
Physical Aspects
Vocal Aspects

Special Strengths

Special Weaknesses

The Life and Death of Our Lakes
Marie Ransley

1. "Warning: the green slime is here."

2. It sounds like a creature out of a grade-B horror movie. But unfortunately it's more real than that. The *New York Times Magazine* warns:

> . . . a monster has been loosed among us. In . . . countless incidents around the world, one can almost hear the sloshing of the algae as they grow and expand like the mucid mutations of the late night horror movies, crawling everywhere and smothering life beneath the slime of cells gone berserk.

3. Yes, algae is the monster, and the immediate victims are our country's lakes.

4. Here in Madison we hear from time to time a plea to "save Madison's lakes." This may be puzzling to people who can't see what danger is threatening the lakes. We don't have a paper or steel industry to pour sludge into them, and the only real problems seem to be a bumper crop of lakeweed and a surface covering of smelly, green scum. But those are just plants. Do we have to save a lake from plants?

5. It's true that algae and lakeweed are natural signs of the normal aging process of lakes. But this process—called eutrophication—can be greatly accelerated by man. And in so doing, man reduces the amount of time the lakes will be enjoyable to him. What I want to talk about today is first the aging process itself, and second, how man accelerates it.

6. The aging process is shown in three types of lakes. The youngest kind is known as oligotrophic, from Greek words which mean "little nourishment." Such a lake has very clear water and contains dissolved oxygen to great depths. It has relatively little organic matter, and so decomposition creates no problem. Production of nutritive materials may exactly equal reduction, and the lake stays clean. It's a closed cycle. In other cases, it's not quite equal; the decomposable material eventually becomes more than the lake can handle, and the lake's condition worsens. The lake progresses to the second stage—eutrophic.

7. A eutrophic lake is, literally, "well fed." The reduction of organic matter through decomposition can't keep pace with production, and the lake tends to become filled: the inevitable result of having too much to eat. The lake is clogged with algae and lakeweed. When this vegetation does decompose, it consumes the deep-water oxygen. The depths of the lake stagnate, making it uninhabitable for cold-water fish which need deep water in the summertime. The lake may have more fish than before, but the fish are apt to be of a less choice species, such as carp.

8. The process continues, and the lake could be called senile. The scientific name for this stage is dystrophic, or "badly fed." Perhaps a better term would be "massively overfed." Nutritive material has accumulated to such an extent that the lake can't digest it at all. The water is oxygen-poor, brownish, and acid. Only a few species can live it it. The undecomposed matter rapidly builds up the lake's shores and fills in its basins. The lake becomes a marsh and then dry land.

9. Good examples of dystrophic lakes are the bog lakes in northern Wisconsin. Now, this area is still relatively unspoiled; the death of these lakes had to come about through natural processes. But elsewhere the process is working a little faster or much faster with man's help.

10. Man's contribution to the eutrophication process is largely through the addition of phosphorus and nitrogen compounds to the drainage system. Of these two, limnologists, or lake scientists, consider phosphorus the bigger troublemaker. But both elements, when poured into the water in heavy concentrations, serve as plant nutrients, and algae, the green slime, take over. The lake becomes eutrophic long before its natural time, and it will die long before its natural time.

11. These phosphorus and nitrogen compounds find their way into the lake from two major sources: sewage and the run-off of water from higher ground. The problem is worsened by man's alterations of the drainage system, through filling in of the marshes.

12. Sewage may be either human or industrial; while the industrial waste isn't as big a problem here in Madison, the human sewage is. Madison is the second fastest growing metropolitan area in the northeast, and the sewage company is busy cleaning up after the two hundred thousand-plus people in Madison and some half a dozen suburbs. Add to this the fact that most of these two hundred thousand people do their wash with phosphate detergents. And add to this the fact that Madison's sewage treatment plant is, like most, only constructed for secondary treatment: it would take a third stage of treatment to remove the phosphates and nitrates. Madison's solution has been not to release the sewage into the water until after bypassing the lakes. This helps the lakes, but doesn't do a lot of good for the rest of the Yahara and Rock River system.

13. The second major source of these nutritive materials is the run-off which flows into the lakes. Urban run-off is apt to be rich in phosphates and nitrates. Some of you know of Starkweather Creek, which flows into Lake

Monona from the east side of Madison. Before the water even gets into the lake, it's caked with green scum.

14. But even harder on the lakes is the agricultural run-off. Dairy farmers in the Madison area keep about 100 cows per square mile. Each one of these cows produces fifteen tons of manure per year. The manure is good nutritive material, and the soil can retain a lot of it, and everything is fine for most of the year. But in winter, when those thousands of cows are still very much alive and digesting, most farmers lack the incentive and the proper storage tanks to store the manure, and so they spread it on top of the snow. The nutrients can't get into the frozen soil, and the spring run-off carries them right down to the lake. Forty-two percent of the phosphorus in Madison's lakes comes from these picturesque dairy farms.

15. Keeping the marshes which surround the lakes would alleviate some of this problem, since marshes work like sponges in soaking up nutrients. It has been said that the remaining marshes around Lake Waubesa are all that are saving that lake. But those marshes won't be there much longer, if some housing developers have their way.

16. In all these ways—sewage, polluted run-off, and landfill—man accelerates the eutrophication process in terms of millennia. Scientists estimate that Lake Erie has aged 15,000 years since 1920. And Madison's Lake Mendota is believed to be in worse shape than Lake Erie. Thus there is reason to hear the plea "Save Madison's lakes!" What a pity it would be if we, in our unthinking way, caused the early death of Madison's lovely lakes. The green slime is caused here.[22]

David: And a Whole Lot of Other Neat People
By Kathy Weisensel

1. There is a problem which is shared by millions of people in the United States. It knows no barrier to age, sex, or social class. Yet, it is a problem that for years was hidden in society's darkest closet. Only recently has the closet door begun to open. That problem is mental retardation.

2. One out of thirty-three persons is born mentally retarded. It is the most widespread, permanent handicap among children. It is among the least understood handicaps of adults. In Wisconsin alone, there are 120,000 retarded people.

3. My involvement with mental retardation has been lifelong and deeply personal. For you see, David, my older brother, is mentally retarded.

4. As our family adjusted to David's problem, we became aware of a number of misconceptions which cloud the public's vision. Among these misconceptions are: that mentally retarded people are mentally ill and therefore dangerous; that mentally retarded people are ineducable; and that mentally retarded people are incapable of leading happy and productive lives. Since these misconceptions are socially harmful and painful to the retarded and their families, it is important that they be corrected.

5. How do you correct the notion that retarded people are somewhat crazy and therefore not really to be trusted? It may be helpful to start with a definition. According to Dr. E. Milo Pritchett, "Mental retardation is a condition of impaired, incomplete, or inadequate mental development. . . . Mental retardation is NOT mental illness. Mental illness is a breakdown of mental functions which were once normal. Specialized care and treatment may restore the person to normalcy. Retardation is a condition for which there is no cure."

6. But let's extend that definition with a series of contrasts. Mental retardation is always permanent; mental illness is usually temporary. Mental retardation is subnormal intelligence; mental illness is distorted intelligence. Mental retardation involves deficient cognitive abilities; mental illness involves emotional impairment of cognitive abilities. Mental retardation is manifested early; mental illness may occur anytime in life. The mentally retarded person is behaviorally stable; it is the mentally ill person who is given to erratic behavior. The extremely mentally retarded person is submissive and mute; the extremely mentally ill person may be violent and criminally dangerous. Thus, retarded people are retarded, and no more. We need no longer place them in pens with the criminally insane, as was the custom in medieval societies.

7. OK, the skeptic says, so what if they aren't mentally ill—they're still ineducable. Those who favor this misconception have, in the words of Dorly D. Wang, formerly of Woods School in Pennsylvania, "one-dimensional views of the retarded." They fail to "distinguish degrees of retardation" and tend to perceive "all the retarded with one image"—and that image is of the intellectual vegetable, more appropriately planted in a cell or ward than in the school classroom. But retarded people are not all alike. Most psychologists identify three subgroups of mentally retarded people: the educable, the trainable, and the custodial.

8. The educable mentally retarded have IQ's ranging from 75 to 50. In the nation's schools, they are placed in a curriculum with a special classroom base, but are encouraged to enter the curricular mainstream whenever it is possible. Most of these students share with normal students instruction in home economics, physical education, shop, and music.

9. The trainable mentally retarded's I.Q. is usually 50 to 30. In the schools, these students are not found in any normal classes. Rather, they work exclusively in special classrooms under the direction of teachers who understand their needs. In these classes, they learn self-care, and they train for social and economic usefulness. Three percent of the present school population is made up of the educable and trainable mentally retarded.

10. The custodial mentally retarded have IQ's below 30. They are usually confined to institutions such as Central Colony, just across Lake Mendota from this University. These people experience little mental development. Few exceed the intellectual acuity of a normal three year old.

11. Thus, the mentally retarded are not a faceless, hopeless mass. While not all of them may profit from schooling, many will. Careful and loving teachers will eventually be rewarded by what one teacher of the retarded has called "the smile of recognition."

12. But to say that the mentally retarded person is not mentally ill and is not ineducable is not enough. It does not destroy the myth that one must be of average mentality to be socially productive and happy. In a society characterized by speed, change, competition, and progress, it is difficult for us so-called "normals" to understand that retarded people can live happily and productively in a life pattern alien to our own.

13. Bernard Posner, Deputy Executive Secretary of the President's Committee on Employment of the Handicapped, has captured society's dilemma in coming to grips with the mentally handicapped. He commented:

> . . . ours are norms in which change is a way of life. In the United States, we change jobs every five years and homes every seven years. We say that to stand still is to regress. Where do the retarded fit in, those without the capacity for constant change?
>
> . . . ours are norms of competition. We compete in school, at play, at love, at work. Where do the retarded fit in, those who can go to school, can play, can love, can work, but who cannot always come out on top in competition?
>
> . . . ours are norms of discontent. Life becomes a series of stepping-stones leading who knows where? Each of life's situations is not to be enjoyed for itself, but is to be tolerated because it leads elsewhere. Where do the retarded fit in, those who can be happy with a stay-put existence?

14. But retarded people do fit in and do lead useful and rewarding lives. A few years ago, I worked with a girl who is educably mentally retarded. Mary went to my high school and attended two normal classes—home economics and physical education. She had a driving desire to become a waitress. Her determination was evident as I tutored her in addition, subtraction, making change, and figuring sales tax. She is working today in a small restaurant—happy and self-supporting.

15. My brother David is another example. Under Wisconsin law, he was entitled to school until age twenty-one, and he spent all those years in a separate special class. There he learned the basic skills of reading, writing and mathematics. After graduation he was employed by the Madison Opportunity Center, a sheltered workshop for the retarded. He leaves home each morning on a special bus and returns each evening after eight hours of simple assembly-line work. While he is by no means self-supporting and independent, he loves his work, and he is a happy man and a neat person with whom to share a family.

16. As a final example, I give you Jeff, age 14. He is custodially mentally retarded at Central Colony. In the three years that I have worked with him, I have found him to be incredibly happy and content in his "permanent childhood." He enjoys toys, writing letters of the alphabet, and watching Sesame Street. This last summer he was especially proud to be selected as a

jumper in the Special Olympics. To tell you the truth, he was chosen because he was one of the few kids in the ward who could get both feet off the floor at the same time. But Jeff doesn't know that the competition wasn't keen, and he's proud and happy.

17. While misconceptions are slow to pass away, they must surely die. Our nation's retarded are not mentally ill, totally ineducable, or incapable of happy and productive lives. I know, in a deeply personal way, the pain that these misconceptions inspire. But I also know that the world is changing. I have a deep faith that you and others of our generation will reject the senseless and destructive stereotypes of the past. As Bernard Posner has said:

> . . . the young people of the world seem to be forging a new set of values. It appears to be a value system of recognizing the intrinsic worth of all humans, retarded or not . . . a value system of acceptance: of accepting life as it is, and people as they are.

18. Thank you for your acceptance.[23]

EXERCISES

UTILIZATION

20. Analyze the preceding speeches using the informative speech evaluation form. You may omit the section on delivery. All other categories should be analyzed.

UTILIZATION

21. Prepare and deliver a four to five minute informative speech that meets the criteria implicit in the informative speech evaluation form.

Notes

1. Otis M. Walter, *Speaking to Inform and Persuade* (New York: Macmillan Co., 1966), p. 4.

2. John F. Wilson and Carroll C. Arnold, *Public Speaking as a Liberal Art* (Boston: Allyn and Bacon, Inc., 1968), pp. 186–87.

3. Ronee Ross, "The Food Stamp Controversy," Unpublished Manuscript, University of Wisconsin, 1975.

4. James N. Rowe, "An American Prisoner of War in South Vietnam," in Wil A. Linkugel, R. R. Allen and Richard L. Johannesen, *Contemporary American Speeches,* 3d ed. (Belmont, Cal.: Wadsworth, 1972), pp. 57–58.

5. Tom Johnson, "Unemployment 1976," Unpublished Manuscript, University of Wisconsin, 1976.

6. William Banowsky, "Persistence and Determination," *Vital Speeches* 41 (1 March 1975): 308.

7. Lauralee Peters, "What Is Totalitarianism?" in Wil Linkugel, R. R. Allen, Richard L. Johannesen, *Contemporary American Speeches,* 2d ed. (Belmont, Cal.: Wadsworth, 1969), pp. 53–54.

8. Felipe Ponce, "La Causa," in Linkugel, et al., *American Speeches,* 3d ed., p. 68.

9. Patricia Ann Hayes, "Madame Butterfly and the Collegian," *Winning Orations* (1967): 8.

10. T. S. Eliot, *Collected Poems 1909–1962* (New York: Harcourt Brace & World, Inc., 1963) pp. 29-31. Copyright © by T. S. Eliot 1963 and 1936 by Harcourt, Brace, & World.

11. Nancy Strom, "Plants Have Feelings," Unpublished Manuscript, University of Wisconsin, 1975.

12. Henry Kissinger, "A New National Partnership," *Vital Speeches* 41 (15 February 1975): 258.

13. Adlai Stevenson, "A Premeditated Attempt: The Building of the Sites," in Linkugel et al., *American Speeches,* 3d ed., pp. 96–97.

14. Joseph Palmer, "Africa: Continent for Change," in Linkugel et al., *American Speeches,* 3d ed., p. 36.

15. Greg Cairns, "Sneaking Sissyism," Unpublished Manuscript, University of Wisconsin, 1974.

16. Elizabeth Langer, "An Instrument of Revelation," in Linkugel et al., *American Speeches,* 3d ed., pp. 302–3.

17. Nancy K. Frank, "Waupun World," Unpublished Manuscript, University of Wisconsin, 1975.

18. Robert J. Havighurst, "The American Family," *Vital Speeches* 14 (1 July 1948): 565.

19. Johnstone G. Patrick, "The Problem of Power," *Vital Speeches* 41 (1 March 1975): 303.

20. Martin Luther King, Jr., "Love, Law, and Civil Disobedience," in Linkugel, et al., *American Speeches,* 3d ed., p. 73.

21. Abstracted from Ellen Berscheid and Elaine Walster, "A Little Bit about Love," in T. L. Huston, ed., *Foundations of Interpersonal Attraction* (New York: Academy Press, 1974), p. 356. Lawrence Durrell, *Clea* (New York: E. P. Dutton, 1961), p. 106. Copyright © 1960 by Lawrence Durrell.

22. Marie Ransley, "The Life and Death of Our Lakes," in Linkugel et al., *American Speeches,* 3d ed., pp. 63–66.

23. Kathy Weisensel, "David: And a Whole Lot of Other Neat People," Unpublished Manuscript, University of Wisconsin, 1976.

6

persuasive speaking

learning objectives

By the conclusion of this chapter you will be able to:

1. Identify four guidelines for stating propositions.

2. Match the names of the guidelines with their descriptions.

3. Identify violations of guidelines in sample propositions.

4. Modify improperly stated propositions to render them satisfactory.

5. Identify two criteria for choosing contentions in support of propositions.

6. Match the two criteria for choosing contentions with their appropriate definitions.

7. Select from a list of contentions those which satisfy the criteria for choosing contentions.

8. Correctly phrase a proposition of your choice and select appropriate supporting contentions.

9. Identify three tests of testimony, three tests of specific instances, and three tests of statistics.

10. Match labels of evidential tests with descriptions of the tests.

11. Identify violations of evidential tests by type.

12. Choose from available evidence that which best supports a given outline.

13. Analyze the use of evidence in a sample speech fragment.

14. Create a one to two minute speech on a proposition of your choice, properly utilizing all three kinds of evidence.

Recall
Comprehension
Application
Analysis
Synthesis

15. Identify four strategies for building credibility.

16. Match strategies for building credibility with descriptions of strategies.

17. Identify sample credibility-building strategies by type.

18. Analyze the use of credibility-building devices in sample speeches.

19. Construct speech introductions utilizing at least two credibility-building strategies.

20. Identify at least three motives and three emotions mentioned in the text.

21. Select from a list of descriptions those which characterize motives and emotions.

22. Identify the motive or emotional appeal used in sample paragraphs.

23. Analyze the use of appeals to motives and emotions in a sample speech fragment.

24. Construct a one to two minute speech appealing to a specific motive or emotion.

25. Analyze sample speeches using a persuasive speech evaluation form.

26. Prepare and deliver a persuasive speech that meets the requirements of the persuasive speech evaluation form.

> Ten expositors purporting to give an account of the nature of atomic fission should not vary too greatly in the substance of their utterance. If they do, either some of them should not be speaking, or the status of contemporary knowledge about atomic fission is one of scandalous disarray. Ten persuaders taking a position on the banning of nuclear weapons testing may appropriately take widely varied positions, and the substance of their utterance would be expected to vary widely.[1]
>
> Donald K. Smith

While informative speaking is important, it would be a very dull and static world indeed were discourse limited to the presentation of that which is known. Advancements in knowledge and constructive social change demand that speakers address themselves to the contingent and the controversial.

In the headnote to this chapter, Donald K. Smith noted an important difference between expositors and persuaders. Responsible informative speakers addressing the same topic ought to present information that is strikingly similar. They must do so if they are to meet the informative requirements: accuracy, completeness, and unity. However, responsible persuasive speakers, operating in the realm of the contingent and the controversial, ought to take positions that vary widely. Such controversy is vital to enlightened decision making in a free society.

In attempting to influence others, we present specific information, just as we do in speeches designed to impart knowledge. A difference between informative and persuasive discourse lies in the use of supporting materials. If they are used to create understanding of an idea or event, the intent is *informative;* if they are used to influence perceptions of what should be thought or done about an idea or event, the intent is *persuasive.*[2] It is not claimed that these categories of intent are mutually exclusive. Speakers often both inform and persuade in a single message.

This chapter is based on the premise that college students care about significant issues and seek to influence the course of human thought and action. The first part of this chapter will help you to phrase your persuasive goals with precision and to determine the ideational requirements of your message. The three parts that follow will consider the persuasive impact of using evidence, building your credibility, and appealing to audience motives and emotions.

Persuading Others: Initial Considerations

As you begin preparation for a persuasive speech, you are likely to ask yourself such questions as: What do I want my audience members to believe or do as a result of my message? and What are the major lines of argument that I must advance to win audience belief or action? This section will help to answer such questions.

Stating the Persuasive Proposition

As you set out to persuade an audience, you will find it helpful to state your central idea with care. The simple declarative sentence that identifies the central idea of a persuasive speech is called the *proposition.* It identifies, in a precise way, your major persuasive goal. The four guidelines that follow will enable you to specify your goal with clarity.

The proposition should contain a single idea. A proposition that advocates a number of areas of belief or courses of action may both confuse your audience and cause your analysis to be imprecise. The propositions that follow are guilty of a multiple focus:

> The United States should institute programs for conserving energy and exploring space.
>
> American colleges offer inadequate preparation for careers and produce students who can't write.

In both of these instances, the proposition focuses on two central ideas. The efforts of the persuasive speaker would be focused better had the speaker narrowed the proposition to one of the two components:

> The United States should institute programs for conserving energy.
>
> The United States should institute programs for exploring space.
>
> American colleges offer inadequate preparation for careers.
>
> American colleges produce students who can't write.

The proposition should be specific. Speakers often phrase their central ideas in vague or general terms. A proposition ought to identify, in a specific way, what is to be believed or what action is to be taken. The propositions that follow are ambiguous:

> Something ought to be done about intercollegiate athletics.
> There is too much sexism in American society.

Both of these propositions may be improved by specifying in concrete ways what the audience is to believe or do.

> Post-season athletic competition should be abolished.
> Elementary-school textbooks are sexist.

The proposition should be expressed as a simple sentence. Persuasive speakers often seek to pack too much information into their propositions. For the moment, you should not be concerned with why the proposition should be affirmed, but only with the belief or action that is sought. The following go beyond the preferable simple sentence:

> You should buy an American car because parts are easier to get, your purchase will stimulate our economy, and American cars are more reasonably priced for what you get.

> Prostitution should be legalized in America to reduce disease, sex crimes, frustration, and loneliness.

In each of these instances, the proposition goes beyond the simple declaration of the proposition. The idea to be affirmed is captured by the simple sentence:

> You should buy an American car.

> Prostitution should be legalized in America.

The proposition should be phrased in clear language. Speakers often beg the question by phrasing their propositions in heavily loaded terms. The propositions that follow reflect this shortcoming.

> Bullyboy politicians of the McCarthy stripe are demagogues skilled in the exploitation of fear.

> The brave American Indian has become the hapless puppet of the American system of wealth distribution.

Although the language of these propositions invites a visceral involvement, it obscures rather than clarifies the proof requirements of the speaker's persuasive goal. What is a bullyboy politician? What is a demagogue? What is it to be skilled in the exploitation of fear? What is a brave American Indian? What is a hapless puppet? And, for that matter, what is a system of wealth distribution? Your analysis of the specific requirements for propositional acceptance may be enhanced by specifying your goals in concrete and definable terms.

> Senator Joseph McCarthy appealed to the American fear of communism.

American Indians have a lower standard of living than do other Americans.

Although it is impossible to phrase propositions in terms that have the same meaning for all members of an audience, ambiguous terms should be avoided. When an ambiguous term is necessary in a proposition, the speaker must be sure to clarify the meaning of the word early in the speech.

Analyzing the Proof Requirements of Your Proposition

Once you have stated your proposition in a clear and precise manner, you must consider the proof requirements of your proposition from the point of view of your audience. In judging the acceptability of your proposition, the members of your audience are likely to question the *relevance* and the *significance* of the supporting ideas you advance. Relevance suggests that the idea or reason *pertains* to the general proposition; significance suggests that the reason is an *important* one—its omission may leave the audience with more questions than answers.

Let us imagine that you wish to affirm the proposition that "The Abominable Snowman Lives." What kinds of specific questions are members of a general audience likely to raise? Most Americans would probably assume that the following questions are both relevant and significant:

Has he (perhaps he is a she) been seen by anyone?

Do experts think such a creature could exist?

Are there any signs of habitation in the area in which the creature is reported to have been seen?

If you answer yes to each of these questions, and you support your answers with evidence, should you expect audience approval? What would be the result if you argued that the Abominable Snowman lives because "he has never been found dead." Most audiences would regard this as an irrelevant factor. On the other hand, how likely would acceptance be if you omitted consideration of the initial question? Reports, perhaps even photographs, are crucial in demonstrating that a creature such as the Abominable Snowman lives. Hopefully, you can support your proposition by answering these questions and not be forced to locate the creature, wrestle it into submission, handcuff it, and drag it behind you to the speaker's stand.

Once you have phrased your proposition clearly and have analyzed your proposition in terms of the questions that your audience members are likely to raise, you are well on the way to preparing your persuasive speech. If your analysis meets the requirements of relevance and significance, you need only to provide support for each of the contentions (lines of argument) that your analysis suggests. In the Abominable Snowman example, your speech will probably unfold as follows:

Proposition: The Abominable Snowman Lives.

I. A number of people have seen the Abominable Snowman.
   A. Support
   B. Support
   C. Support
   D. Support

II. Many respected anthropologists say the creature could exist.
   A. Support
   B. Support
   C. Support

III. Numerous signs that a creature exists can be found in the region in which the creature was spotted.
   A. Support
   B. Support
   C. Support
   D. Support
   E. Support

IV. The creature has been "captured" on film for all to see.
   A. Support
   B. Support
   C. Support

Notice that your most convincing *contention* has been saved for last. After you have shown your 35-mm slides and your 8-mm sound film, hopefully you will have eliminated the last shred of doubt. Notice also how your audience's questions have been converted to *contentions* —declarative sentences that support the acceptance of your proposition.

Another example will help to demonstrate that the contentions you should advance in support of your proposition are influenced by the particular audience you are addressing. Imagine that you are vice-president of Towers, Inc., a construction firm that specializes in high-rise buildings. Your company wishes to build a twenty-five-story office building on the outskirts of Fair Prairie, a suburban community. The building will be twenty stories higher than any other structure in the community. A "variance," or exception to existing building codes, will have to be granted before work can begin.

You have been asked by the Fair Prairie Building Commission to appear at a hearing that will be open to all interested citizens. Having read back issues of the local newspaper, *The Prairie Wind,* you are aware that your proposed building is a source of controversy in the community. Individual businessowners fear that your structure will divert business from the central section of the city to its outskirts. A local environmental group, Save Our Swamp (SOS), is concerned about the impact of your building on the natural drainage system. The editor of *The Prairie Wind* has said it will ruin the architectural integrity of the community. The chief of the fire department questions its safety since the tallest portable ladder owned by the department reaches only five stories.

Given your awareness of these issues, what contentions would appear to be relevant and significant? Consider the following:

Proposition: A variance permitting construction of Prairie Towers should be granted.

- I. Prairie Towers will favorably influence all segments of the Fair Prairie economy.
  - A. It will provide jobs for Fair Prairie residents.
    1. Support
    2. Support
  - B. It will stimulate all areas of the present business community.
    1. Support
    2. Support
  - C. It will broaden the community tax base.
    1. Support
    2. Support
- II. Prairie Towers will provide for environmental protection.
  - A. The Prairie Tower Complex provides for the preservation of natural forests, grasslands, and marsh lands.
    1. Support
    2. Support
  - B. The Prairie Tower Complex will save the area from suburban sprawl.
    1. Support
    2. Support
- III. Prairie Towers will be an aesthetically attractive structure.
  - A. It will be characterized by long, clean lines.
    1. Support
    2. Support
  - B. It will be surrounded by greenlands and waterways.
    1. Support
    2. Support
- IV. Prairie Towers will be a functionally sound building.
  - A. It will contain the very latest safety devices.
    1. Support
    2. Support

B. Service and support facilities will be an integral part of the building.
   1. Support
   2. Support

As a representative of Towers, Inc., you have anticipated the criteria that will be used by varied segments of the Fair Prairie community in judging the wisdom of the code variance. While you may not have anticipated all of the questions that citizens may raise at the hearing, you have shown yourself to be sensitive to the broad concerns of the community. Given this basic presentation, you may answer other specific questions as they emerge in the forum period.

EXERCISES

VERIFICATION

1. Identify the four guidelines for stating propositions.
   a.
   b.
   c.
   d.

VERIFICATION

2. Match the four guidelines above with the descriptions that follow. (Caution: one of the descriptions does not apply.) You may abbreviate the guidelines.
   a. ____________ The proposition is phrased in nonemotive, easily definable language.
   b. ____________ The proposition expresses only one thought.
   c. ____________ The proposition is not stated in complex form.
   d. ____________ The proposition may be phrased as a rhetorical question.
   e. ____________ The proposition identifies a concrete thought or action.

UTILIZATION

3. Indicate, in abbreviated language, the guidelines being violated in each of the samples presented below. If none of the guidelines is violated, write "none" in the space provided.

a. ______________________ Americans should buckle up for safety to reduce the hazards of broken limbs caused by auto accidents.

b. ______________________ Bubble-headed professors sympathetic to commie pinkos should be banned from campus.

c. ______________________ The postal service should be returned to cabinet-level status within the executive branch of government.

d. ______________________ Something should be done about the plight of the migrant worker.

e. ______________________ Colleges should institute three-year-degree programs and provide more scholarships for disadvantaged students.

UTILIZATION

4. On a separate sheet of paper, modify each of the improperly stated propositions in question 3 to bring them into conformity with the guidelines for stating propositions. If the proposition is stated satisfactorily, leave it as is.

   a.

   b.

   c.

   d.

   e.

VERIFICATION

5. Identify the two criteria for choosing contentions in support of a proposition.

   a.

   b.

VERIFICATION

6. Match the two criteria in exercise 5 with the definitions that follow. (Caution: one of the definitions does not apply.)

   a. ______________________ The contention induces audience empathy.

   b. ______________________ The contention is of crucial importance.

   c. ______________________ The contention is pertinent to the proposition being advanced.

UTILIZATION

7. Place a check mark next to each of the hypothetical contentions listed below that satisfies the criteria for choosing contentions.
   Proposition: The standard of living of American Indians is substandard.
   a. _____ Indians own fewer television sets than other minority groups.
   b. _____ Average annual income is lower for Indians than it is for other segments of the population.
   c. _____ Most Indians live on a diet weak in protein.
   d. _____ Indians in the southwest have a higher standard of living than do Indians in the northwest.
   e. _____ Many Indians still live in substandard housing.
   f. _____ Many Indians still live on reservations.
   g. _____ Indians subscribe to fewer magazines than do other segments of the population.
   h. _____ The death rate among Indians is higher than for other segments of the population.

UTILIZATION

8. Select a proposition of your choice; phrase it in accordance with the guidelines for stating propositions; and list supporting reasons that satisfy the criteria for choosing contentions.

   Proposition:

   Contentions:

   1.

   2.

   3.

   4.

Supporting Your Arguments with Evidence

Having stated your proposition and having identified your key contentions, you are now ready to marshall evidence in support of your arguments. Aristotle noted that there are only two essential parts of a speech: the statement of what is to be proved and the proof itself. In this section, we will consider three kinds of evidence that speakers use to support their contentions: testimony, specific instances, and statistics.

Testimony

Speakers often use quotations or testimonials from qualified people to justify the arguments they advance. One student supported the proposition that grades are not useful motivational factors in stimulating the work of elementary school children by citing the testimony of two social scientists:

> Hilgard and Russell concluded that "most marking systems are undesirable forms of motivation in that they stem from the authority of the teacher or principal rather than from the relationship between skills, attitudes, or information acquired and the motivational system of the pupil. They are often dangerous in that they limit outstanding success to the few, and if based on actual achievement, condemn a large group of children to continued frustration and defeat in school." [3]

Taken in the context of the speaker's overall proposition—that grades should be abolished in elementary schools—the testimony offered provides compelling reasons to question the continuation of present grading practices.

However, the practices of the American advertising industry have taught us that testimony is not always a logical cause for belief: Joe Namath endorsed pantyhose; Danny Thomas endorsed coffee makers; Jane Powell endorsed exercisers. To ensure that your testimony is deserving of belief, you will find it helpful to ask yourself the following questions:

Was the source of the testimony in a position to observe the situation being reported? If a friend told you, "Boy, the Buckaroos played a lousy game last night" and you later discovered that your friend hadn't seen the basketball game, would your willingness to accept the statement be diminished? Similarly, someone who insists that a coach should be fired because the team is losing but hasn't been to a single game, is not in a very favorable position to render a verdict. It isn't always reasonable to demand that a source has personally witnessed an event. For example, we don't expect that our local "weatherperson" flies to Canada every afternoon to witness the progress of an impending cold front. Sources of testimony may also be in a position to observe if they have access to relevant information upon which to draw in making responsible, reliable judgments.

Is the source of the testimony competent to judge? A person can be in a position to observe, but may nevertheless be an incompetent judge of events. Social scientists may lack the necessary skills to interpret the data they gather. Weatherpersons may be incompetent as judges of meteorological information. Certain kinds of judgments require expertise. When special qualifications are essential to informed testimony, you must ensure that your source has sufficient expertise and, of course, expertise is not transferable from one field to another.

Is the source of the testimony biased? In a speech favoring agricultural subsidies, you present testimony from the chairman of the Senate Agriculture Committee. Later, an audience member points out that the senator receives a cash subsidy each year from the program his testimony supported. Do you suppose the "proof value" of your citation has been weakened? Anytime the source has a personal stake in the outcome, the testimony is suspect.

Two questions students often raise regarding the presentation of testimony are: (1) How much information about the source should I present? and (2) How do I introduce and end a verbatim citation? While there are no fixed rules, the amount of source qualifications presented can be a function of audience familiarity with and attitude toward the source used. If the audience has never heard of Dr. Anthrax, they have no way of assessing his or her qualifications. Thus, a brief reference to a person's position or training would dispel doubt. If audience members are familiar with the source and regard him or her negatively, care should be taken to illustrate why the source should be believed in *this* particular instance. The second question refers to a matter of style. Generally, you should lead into citations naturally: "As Senator Mike Mansfield observed. . . ." At the end, a statement summarizing the importance of the citation may be used to indicate that you are no longer quoting: "Senator Mansfield's statement leads us to believe that. . . ." The use of "Quote . . . Unquote" is a stilted, unnatural device for introducing and ending citations.

Specific Instances

Your hypothetical friend might, if challenged, back up the claim "The coach should be fired" by offering the testimony of several important sports officials and players. Your friend also might cite instances in which the coach allowed members of the team to break training rules, showed poor judgment in substituting players, and caused his players to suffer mental anguish. In so doing, your friend would be citing specific instances as substantiation of his or her claim.

Mr. Anson Mount, quoted earlier, used several specific instances in supporting his assertion that *Playboy* had become "a significant forum for the discussion and debate of current social issues and moral values":

> Let us look at a few of the articles that have appeared in just the last three issues of *Playboy:* An article on the phenomenon of human genius by Robert Graves; an article about "Hunger in America" by Senator Jacob Javits; "The Americanization of Vietnam" by David Halberstam; an examination of the personality of Jesus and his significance to current social and moral issues by Baptist theologian Harvey Cox. . . .[4]

Mr. Mount listed nine other essays and their authors as further proof of the significance of the magazine. By this accumulation of instances, Mount hoped to impress his Baptist audience that *Playboy* was not a "filthy, porno rag."

When using specific instances, the strength of the accumulated weight of evidence is dependent on positive responses to three questions:

Are the instances cited representative? In order for specific instances to have persuasive impact, the audience must see them as representative examples of the assertion in question. With respect to Mr. Mount's listing of essays, some audience members may have wondered how many "low quality" essays and stories could be found in the issues cited, and whether or not the last three issues were truly representative of the magazine's contribution. If the instances of a coach's indiscretions and violations are unrepresentative of his actions and attributes, an unfair picture was painted by your hypothetical friend.

Are the instances sufficient in number? If you polled your class on the question "Should a Coke machine be put in the library?" and received only three replies (out of a possible twenty-five), could you claim that the class supported the request? Probably not. The instances, even assuming all three were favorable, are not sufficient justification for your claim. Although there is no "magic number" of instances that you must have, you must nevertheless be concerned about how many you need in order to support your point. In Mr. Mount's case, twelve instances from only three issues would seem sufficient to justify the claim that *Playboy* treated significant social and moral issues.

Are there negative instances that should be accounted for? If negative instances, those contrary to the claim or opposite of those used, are apparent to the audience, the speaker's position is seriously weakened. A speaker may assert, "Burglary is rising in the suburbs of this city." If the number of burglaries has fallen in one or two suburbs, this would be sufficient to qualify the generalization. If there are only three suburbs, then the force of the negative instances becomes even greater.

Specific instances, while vulnerable to attack, may render an argument vivid and concrete by showing that the generalization influences flesh and blood human beings functioning in real life situations. For this reason, specific instances are often used. in conjunction with testimony and statistics to ensure that the social impact of the generalization may be visualized by the audience.

Statistics

Numerical means are often used to substantiate a proposition: "There were thirty cases of influenza this year; this was ten more than last year—an increase of fifty percent. This city should stock up on influenza vaccine." Examples of the use of statistics to support ideas are numerous. One student used comparative numerical data to support the contention that cable television stations should be allowed to buy wire capable of transmitting twelve channels rather than twenty, as currently required:

> Shielded twenty-channel copper-based cable lists for $5,702 per mile, as compared to the cable with only twelve channel capabilities at $4,799. For a new operator buying 100 miles of cable, the difference is substantial: $90,300.[5]

Brent Simmons incorporated the citation of specific instances with statistical data to support his proposal for more Black economic power:

> The "Harlem Co-op" supermarket was created by the initial investment of $160,000 from 3,785 Black residents. It now averages $39,000 worth of business weekly and pays cash dividends to its shareholders. . . . The most impressive example of "black capitalism" at work

> is "Progress Plaza" in Philadelphia, which is perhaps the largest shopping center in the world, owned and operated by Blacks with assets of over $4 million.[6]

James T. Needham underscored the significance of the economic crisis in this nation by citing a statistic from the New York Stock Exchange's study "of the capital needs and savings potential of the U.S. economy through 1985":

> I don't want to burden you with a lot of statistics this morning. Our full report will be available to everyone who may wish to study it. But one number leaps out of that report and looms very ominously on the national economic horizon.
>
> That number is 650 billion—and it represents the projected gap between the domestic supply of investment expected to be available between 1974 and 1985, and the amount of investment capital that—in the absence of a gift from heaven—will be needed to meet our national economic requirements.
>
> $650 billion. It's easy enough to toss off that kind of figure without focusing on what it represents or could accomplish. Well, what could $650 billion do if it were put to a single use?
>
> In terms that are closest to this great city, $650 billion could buy two new automobiles for every family in America—with quite a bit left over for fuel and maintenance.
>
> $650 billion could provide decent new housing for the entire populations of New York, Chicago, Los Angeles, Philadelphia, Detroit and the next eight largest cities in America.
>
> $650 billion could feed every man, woman and child in the United States for 2½ years.
>
> $650 billion could do many things. Perhaps more to the point, it could cover between 13 percent and 14 percent of this country's aggregate capital needs between now and 1985.[7]

As you will note, Mr. Needham did not just toss out the figure, $650 billion, as though everyone understood it. Even though his audience, The Economic Club of Detroit, could be presumed to understand economic figures, Needham took time to impress upon the group the massive amount being discussed. Mr. Needham also referred implicitly to a problem most speakers face in using statistics: they may seem a "burden" to the listener, especially when the suggestions for their use (see chapter five) are not heeded.

Statistical data, however, can be misused as easily as it can be used. Thus, a careful scrutiny of "statistical proof" is essential to avoid being duped by a fast-number artist. The crucial and overriding question is: Do these statistics really represent what they are purported to represent?

Is the source reliable? If the poll is taken by the "Fly-by-Night Statistical Survey Service," how reliable is it? Gallup and Roper polls have a history of being fair, judicious estimates of public opinion. Data from a government handbook and from scientific studies reported in professional journals probably are more reliable than those presented in *National Enquirer* or *Public Opinion Magazine*.

Is the statistical data based on an adequate sample? Polling the members of a commune and discovering that 97 percent favor a communal life does not support the proposition: Most college students favor a communal life. This question takes us back to the tests applied to specific instances, particularly the representativeness and sufficiency of the sample.

Is the statistical report misleading? A speaker may present a seemingly complete and accurate picture of a body of data that, in fact, is misleading: "The Soviet Union increases its GNP by 6 percent over last year, while the U.S. increased its GNP by only 4 percent. It is clear that we are falling behind the Soviet Union in production." Actual dollar figures may suggest a different conclusion (hypothetical figures):

USSR G.N.P.		*US G.N.P.*	
Last Year	This Year	Last Year	This Year
$60 Billion	$63.6 Billion	$100 Billion	$104 Billion
+3.6/6 percent		+4.0/4 percent	

In percentage, we appear to be falling behind. In actual dollars, however, we are keeping pace with the Soviet Union. The speaker ignores the difference in bases: $60 billion versus $100 billion. This is only one of several misleading uses of statistical information.[8]

One final thought: in using evidence, a speaker is often advised to present a variety of evidence in support of arguments. Statistics present numerical summaries of vast amounts of data; specific instances provide vivid and concrete examples of the assertion in question; testimony demonstrates that qualified people interpret the statistics and specific instances in the same way that you do. The collective use of these three kinds of evidence can have strong audience impact.

EXERCISES

VERIFICATION

9. Identify the tests of evidence in the order presented in the textbook.

   a. *Testimony*

      1.

      2.

      3.

   b. *Specific Instances*

      4.

      5.

      6.

   c. *Statistics*

      7.

      8.

      9.

VERIFICATION

10. Match the numbers in exercise 9 with the descriptions that follow.

    a. _____ Enough examples are presented.
    b. _____ The source of the statistics should have a good reputation.
    c. _____ Source is an expert, where expertise is required.
    d. _____ Either see it, or have access to data.
    e. _____ Examples which deny the assertion are accounted for.
    f. _____ Person has something to gain.
    g. _____ The numerical tabulation covers a large number of individuals.
    h. _____ Examples are typical.
    i. _____ The numerical statement is clear in meaning.

UTILIZATION

11. Identify the test of evidence that is violated in the following examples. (Caution: one of the examples does not apply; use each test only once.)

a. ______________________________ Just look at Joe Swartz's kid—it's just like I told you, all college students are freaks.

b. ______________________________ Nine out of ten students say they like the instructor; so he must relate well to his students.

c. ______________________________ I don't care if you did see Reverend Blatz drinking beer at a neighborhood picnic—I still say that ministers don't drink.

d. ______________________________ Based on the ten responses to my questionnaire, which was sent to professors all over the country, I can say that 70% of the professors are Democrats.

e. ______________________________ My science teacher says the Navy is going to explode a new secret weapon.

f. ______________________________ After questioning Sierra Club members in each of the 50 states, I have concluded that Americans are overwhelmingly against the killing of wildlife for sport.

g. ______________________________ Bug Tussle is growing 7,000 times faster than San Francisco.

h. ______________________________ The President of the American Medical Association observes that socialized medicine isn't working in England.

i. ______________________________ A radical student group, called Numbers, Inc., has concluded that 95 percent of American corporations have illegal political slush funds.

j. ______________________________ Steve McQueen says the two party system is dead.

UTILIZATION

12. Consider the outline that follows:
Proposition: The U.S. is not facing an energy shortage.

I. Energy supplies are adequate.
   A. Coal supplies are adequate.
   B. Oil supplies are adequate.
   C. Natural gas supplies are adequate.
II. Alternative energy sources are plausible.
   A. Nuclear power is plausible.
   B. Solar energy is plausible.

From the evidence that follows, select the testimony that best supports each of the statements. You should have one piece of evidence for each main point in the outline and one piece of evidence for each supporting point.

a. Frank Golbert, *American Technologist*
   The physical knowledge and technological resources needed to use solar energy on such a scale are now available.

b. *Danforth News*, October 10, 1976
   It is imperative that the U.S. continue to import oil. Our own resources cannot fuel our economy for any substantial length of time.

c. L.A. Stress, Professor of Physics, University of Maine, *Nuclear Energy: A Future Perspective*, 1975, p. 27.
   Using 1975 as a base year, we estimate that by 1985 oil and gas production could be increased by as much as 80% and coal production could be increased by 65%. Clearly, our energy supplies are sufficient. All we need is improved technology and, of course, commitment.

d. *National Energy Index*, October 1975, p. 2.
   The abundance of potentially mineable coal of all grades including low sulphur coal is unquestioned.

e. Rich Granite, Economist, *Long Island Globe*, May 18, 1971, p. 7.
   According to a U.S. survey, the seabed has a potential supply of 2800 billion barrels of oil—enough to supply 40% of the world's energy needs for 23 years.

f. Elmer Elliott, Nuclear Physicist, *The Atomic Journal*, March 6, 1975, p. 8.
   Nuclear Energy is superior to conventional fuels in a number of ways. For example, nuclear power costs less. Also, there is no real limit on the amount of power which can be produced. Finally, nuclear power is clean.

g. *Business Today*, March 16, 1976, p. 13.
   As fuel prices climb, the movement toward garbage power will unquestionably gain in momentum.

h. *The International Globe*, May 12, 1977, p. 2.
   Our domestic natural gas supply could last until 1995 if we practice better conservation.

i. Ray McAllen, Director, The National Power Institute, *National Power Report,* February, 1977, p. 77.
The current discovery rate of oil is so impressive that a 210 year supply has been labeled by geologists as proved reserves.

j. William Williams, *New American Scientist,* June 1974, p. 9.
The oil crisis and massive increases in the price of natural gas have prompted the search for alternative sources of energy.

k. Henry Kissmeyer, *New York World-Dispatch,* September 22, 1975.
The production of oil on the outer continental shelf is less disruptive environmentally than strip mining.

l. Mary Ann Sturdly, Director, University of Montana, Energy Resources Center, *Technical Report,* August 1976, p. 155.
We have the technology to construct solar energy collection sites right now. By the year 2000, solar power could supply over 70% of our nation's energy needs at a substantially reduced cost.

m. Erica Martin, *San Jose Tabloid,* May 1975.
Coal, gas and oil reserves in the U.S. can be expected to increase rapidly over the next few years.

n. William Smith, Office of Energy Development, *American Technologist,* January 1975, p. 43.
A recent staff study has concluded that there are 1.15 quadrillion cubic feet of proven natural gas reserves. That's three times the amount consumed in our nation's entire history.

o. *International Trends Magazine,* June 5, 1975.
Spain will meet the bulk of its electricity energy needs from nuclear plants by 1995.

p. *National Newsletter,* February 12, 1977, p. 202.
Martin Glump of Project Windpower proposes to place a windmill on every house by the year 2020.

q. Ralph Richards, Chairperson, National Power Agency, *Energy Now,* January 19, 1977, p. 55.
Massive research and development efforts have been expended on alternative sources for more than 25 years. Of the alternatives examined, solar and nuclear energy offer the greatest promise from both an environmental and economic perspective.

r. Rose Williams, Geophysicist, *Geothermal Journal,* November 1974, p. 19.
If we used all of the possible sites everywhere in the world, we would meet no more than 1% of the world's present energy needs through tidal power.

s. Marsha White, Professor of Physical Science, University of Texas, *Energy Resource Journal,* March 1976, p. 10.

Recent studies completed at the University of Texas reveal that there are sufficient coal reserves to satisfy all U.S. energy needs, at the present rate of consumption, for 600 years.

t. *World Environment Report,* February 9, 1971.
The process of extracting oil from sand requires vast amounts of water and produces vast quantities of waste matter.

UTILIZATION

13. Analyze the use of evidence provided in the following paragraph.

We need stricter federal regulations controlling the sale of prescription drugs. Writing in a professional journal in 1961, Dr. Walter Modell, associate professor of pharmacology at Cornell University, called attention to glaring problems in the control of drugs. Dr. Modell noted that ". . . excessive numbers of drugs are now being introduced—excessive in view of the working capacities of those competent to test their safety and utility in man, excessive in view of the subjects available for testing their effects, dangers and uses in man, and excessive in view of the ability of those who must assimilate the essential knowledge and learn how to prescribe them effectively and safely." Thirteen years later, in 1974, Dr. Modell was asked to comment on the steps being taken to protect the public from possibly hazardous new drugs. Dr. Modell handed the interviewer a copy of the 1961 article with the cryptic comment: "Nothing has changed." The most glaring instance of a drug being marketed before being fully tested is, of course, thalidomide. Between 1958 and 1962, ten thousand babies were born without arms or legs. Others were deformed in worse ways, grotesque caricatures of human beings. All because of a sleeping pill called thalidomide. But, you might say, this was a world-wide problem—not one caused just by our country's drug control policies. Consider the following example. In 1966 reports were published regarding a cancer vaccine. The drug was put on the market and prescribed by some 200 doctors throughout the country. When the vaccine was further investigated, it was found to contain substances contaminated by bacteria, by a possible residue of benzidrine—which can produce cancer, and by a substance carefully labeled not for humans, but "for chemical and investigative use only" and for "laboratory research on animals." The only effect this drug had on the over 500 patients who received it was to hasten their demise. Are these isolated instances? I think not. In 1966 a total of 178 different drugs were recalled because they were of low or unknown quality. In 1975 the number jumped to 702, almost three times the number recalled in 1966. In this same nine year interval, an estimated 20,000 new drugs were introduced into the market. Half these new drugs were never fully tested before their release. Instead, the manufacturers and physicians used us as patients to determine whether or not the drug was successful. Clearly, we do need tighter controls on the release of drugs.[9]

UTILIZATION

14. Construct a one to two minute speech on a proposition of your choice, utilizing all three kinds of evidence, in such a way that no tests of evidence are violated.

Building Your Credibility

Aristotle, writing centuries before the birth of Christ, observed that the speaker's character may be called "the most effective means of persuasion." [10] We tend to believe those whom we respect, admire, and trust. During the past fifty years, communication researchers have verified the importance of source credibility in winning the favorable acceptance of ideas. In this section, we will consider four strategies that you may use to render yourself more credible as a source of persuasive messages.

Indicate Your Qualifications

The speaker's competence, his or her qualifications to speak on the topic in question, is a significant factor in winning audience belief. We tend to believe those who are "experts" on the topic addressed. At times, speakers find it useful to remind the audience of their special qualifications to speak. In affirming the proposition that rational discourse is declining, Franklyn S. Haiman, a professor of public address at Northwestern University, reminded a college audience in Kansas of his expertise when he noted:

> As one who, in earlier years, has written rather extensively about the ethics of persuasion and who has been identified as a spokesman for the so-called "rational" school of thought, I find my previous reputation in this subject both an advantage and handicap.[11]

Similarly, the late General Douglas MacArthur, addressing an audience of West Point cadets, justified his portrayal of the American fighting man with this allusion to experience:

> In twenty campaigns, on a hundred battlefields, around a thousand campfires, I have witnessed that enduring fortitude, that patriotic self-abnegation, and that invincible determination which have carved his statue in the hearts of his people.[12]

In both instances, the speakers established their qualifications to speak by reference to their backgrounds.

Although student speakers are seldom experts, in the true sense of the word, they often are qualified to speak because of special experience or study. Paul Koeppe invoked his work qualifications when affirming the proposition that "nuclear power is a viable energy option."

> I'm certain that most of you have heard about the attempts to put an end to the nuclear power industry. I have, and it has placed me in an uncomfortable position. I work for a utility company. The charges against nuclear power have caused me to make a personal effort to research the facts. I have looked beyond the literature of the power industry to reports of government agencies, reports of independent investigative agencies, and even reports of the opponents of nuclear power. As a result of my research, I am convinced that nuclear power is a necessary and viable energy resource.[13]

Similarly, David Wheatly, another undergraduate student, drew upon his everyday experiences with a car pool to demonstrate his personal qualifications to speak.

> For several years I was one of the single occupancy drivers, making my solitary way to school each day. I was, like other lonely drivers, spending all my extra cash on gasoline and on car maintenance. Now, that has all changed. For the past eighteen months, I have been in a car pool. From this experience, I have benefited not only financially, but socially as well. So, I'm not here today to toot my own horn. I'm here to honk the horn of the car pool.[14]

In both of these instances, student speakers sought to establish their qualifications by noting the research that they had conducted on the subject or by noting special experiences that had provided insights.

Demonstrate Desirable Personal Qualities

Although a speaker's excellent qualifications may be known to the audience, the speaker may still fail to win consent because he or she appears to be lacking in the personal qualities that the audience finds desirable. Adlai Stevenson spent a professional lifetime trying to overcome the "cold," "egghead" image that American voters seemed to disfavor.

Among the personal qualities that audiences may honor are intelligence, trustworthiness, a sense of humor, humility, dynamism, friendliness, sincerity, compassion, and poise. Different audiences, of course, may honor different personal qualities. Johnny Cash's success with prison audiences may be largely explained by his ability to project toughness, worldliness, and machismo—the personal qualities with which male convicts find it possible to identify. In seeking to persuade, a speaker is well advised to reflect the human attributes that the audience admires and respects.

Let us consider two examples. The first example is taken from a speech, "Who Is Tampering with the Soul of America?", delivered by Jenkin Lloyd Jones, editor of the *Tulsa Tribune,* to the Inland Daily Press Association in Chicago on October 16, 1961. As you read this quotation, consider the personal qualities that Jones reflected.

> It is time we hit the sawdust trail. It is time we revived the idea that there is such a thing as sin—just plain old willful sin. It is time we brought self-discipline back into style. And who has a greater responsibility at this hour than we, the gentlemen of the press?
>
> So I suggest: Let's look to our educational institutions at the local level, and if Johnny can't read by the time he's ready to get married, let's find out why.
>
> Let's look at the distribution of public largesse and if, far from alleviating human misery, it is producing the sloth and irresponsibility that intensifies it, let's get it fixed.
>
> Let's quit being bulldozed and bedazzled by self-appointed longhairs. Let's have the guts to say that a book is dirt if that's what we think of it, or that a painting may well be a daub if you can't figure out which way to hang it. And if some beatnik welds together a collection of rusty cogwheels and old corset stays and claims it's a greater sculpture than Michelangelo's *David,* let's have the courage to say that it looks like junk and probably is.
>
> Let's blow the whistle on plays that would bring blushes to an American Legion stag party. Let's not be awed by movie characters with barnyard morals even if some of them have been photographed climbing aboard the Presidential yacht. Let us pay more attention in our news columns to the decent people everywhere who are trying to do something for the good of others.
>
> In short, gentlemen, let's cover up the cesspool and start planting some flowers.[15]

What personal qualities were reflected? Among those you may have noted are tenacity, toughness, strong sense of morality, dynamism, and earthy humor. This speech was immensely successful with the particular audience addressed. What generalizations can you make about that audience?

The second example is taken from a speech, "Man's Other Society," which was delivered by Richard M. Duesterbeck while he was an undergraduate student at Wisconsin State College-Eau Claire. Early in the speech, Mr. Duesterbeck identified his qualifications to speak about prison reform by noting that he himself was an exconvict. But later in the speech he demonstrated strong personal qualities when he said:

> Now you may be thinking: Well what did he expect? He asked for it, didn't he? And you are right, I got exactly what I deserved. I am ashamed of having done time, but I did; and although I would give my right arm to be able to turn back the pages of time, it cannot be done. . . .
>
> It is easy to stand here and criticize the prison community, especially after one has done time in it. Criticism of this nature, however, bears with it little validity unless the person making the accusation stands ready to propose a program that will eliminate the evils to which he objects.[16]

What personal qualities are demonstrated? He reflected a lack of self-pity as well as the attributes of penitence, maturity, and responsibility. It is difficult to reject the persuasive message of such a man.

Show Good Will Toward the Audience

In addition to demonstrating sound qualifications and desirable personal qualities, speakers also find it worthwhile to show that they respect their audiences and feel good will toward them. When speakers recognize the achievements of their audiences, or express affection or respect for their audiences, audience members are likely to reciprocate in kind. Speaking before the Noise Abatement Council of America, Senator Mark Hatfield recognized the group's efforts in this fashion:

> Your concern with environmental pollution has brought you here today in order to form an effective citizen's group to combat this onslaught on our planet before it is too late. . . . in your recognition of noise as a pollutant you have established yourselves as pioneers in combatting the effects of noise on our society.[17]

This brief recognition conveys an understanding of the group's mission. By appreciating that mission and making the sentiment known, Senator Hatfield increased his credibility rating during the presentation of his speech.

Seek to Reduce Audience Hostility

There are times when a speaker must address an audience that is hostile toward the speaker and/or his message. In such instances, speakers must find ways of reducing hostility so that their messages may gain a fair hearing.

Consider the challenge faced by a representative from *Playboy* speaking at a Southern Baptist Convention. Mr. Anson Mount, Manager of Public Affairs for *Playboy*, responded as follows:

> I am sure we are all aware of the seeming incongruity of a representative of *Playboy* magazine speaking to an assemblage of representatives of the Southern Baptist Convention. I was intrigued by the invitation when it came last fall, though I was not surprised. I am grateful for your genuine and warm hospitality, and I am flattered (though again not surprised) by the implication that I would have something to say that could have meaning to you people. Both *Playboy* and the Baptists have indeed been considering many of the same issues and ethical problems; and even if we have not arrived at the same conclusions, I am impressed and gratified by your openness and willingness to listen to our views.[18]

In beginning his speech, Mr. Mount reduced hostility by openly recognizing the discrepancy in beliefs, by stressing the "common ground" that existed in both parties' concern for the same issues, and by expressing his conviction that his ideas would receive a fair hearing.

When faced with an audience whose beliefs are significantly different from your own, you should consider the three devices that Mr. Mount employed: (1) *recognizing discrepancies between beliefs,* (2) *identifying common ground,* and (3) *using a "fair play" appeal.* While he may not have won many converts to the "Playboy Philosophy," he did his best to insure that his audience would listen to his ideas and judge them on their merits.

Although the introduction of your speech is the most obvious place to utilize the means of building credibility discussed in this section, the audience's assessment of your credibility occurs throughout the presentation. Thus, as Aristotle indicated centuries ago, a speaker should concentrate on enhancing the image being portrayed throughout the speech.

EXERCISES

VERIFICATION

15. Identify the four strategies for building credibility.

    a.

    b.

    c.

    d.

VERIFICATION

16. Match the four strategies for building credibility with the descriptions that follow. (Caution: two of the descriptions do not apply.)

a. ______________________ The speaker indicates his or her high regard for the audience.

b. ______________________ The speaker appeals to the audience's sense of sportsmanlike conduct.

c. ______________________ The speaker perspires profusely.

d. ______________________ The speaker establishes his or her expertise on the subject being discussed.

e. ______________________ The speaker appeals to the fears of the audience.

f. ______________________ The speaker appears humble and sincere.

UTILIZATION

17. Identify the credibility strategy employed in each of the following samples. You may abbreviate the strategies.

Type	*Strategy*
______________	"My six years as a lineman for the O.D. and O.R. Railroad have given me many opportunities to observe safety practices in railroad yards."
______________	"Although I recognize your beliefs are different from my own, I believe I shall obtain a fair hearing from you."
______________	"I have always said that your organization is one of the most important in fighting pollution throughout the land."
______________	"I realize my vast years of experience should give me all the answers to the problem that faces us, but I am still a simple farm boy at heart."

UTILIZATION

18. Analyze the use of specific credibility building devices in the following samples.

a. I am glad to see so many people interested in Cub Scouting here this evening. By way of introduction let me explain that I share your interest, having been in scout work with young boys for over eight years.

During that time I have seen many more good leaders than bad ones but I know that the strength of the program lies in the cooperation between leaders and parents, and I seek your help in that direction. No one has quite the understanding of your young son that you do, and his sound development is another interest that we have in common.
(Mrs. Pat Anderson, Unpublished Manuscript, Madison, 1976.)

b. I am truly honored to have been asked to speak to you on your Honors Day. But to honor you, I must first honor myself by being honest with you. To honor you fully, I feel I must say things to you which much of our society today, apparently, would indict as dishonorable. To honor you properly, I feel I must say things which are seldom said these days—the "unmentionables" within a framework of thinking that has become so deeply established and pervasive that they resound with the tremor of heresy.

For you see, I have just about reached the end of my tolerance for the way our society at the present time seems to have sympathetic concern only for the misfit, the pervert, the drug addict, the drifter, the ne'er-do-well, the maladjusted . . . in general, the underdog. . . . I trust it is sufficiently clear by this time why I am so honored and so pleased to be invited to speak at this honors convocation. This is one of the few remaining ceremonies where the achiever is honored.
(Miller Upton, "If This be Heresy. . . ." *Vital Speeches*, 34 [Nov. 1, 1967], 37.)

UTILIZATION

19. Write a speech introduction that incorporates at least two of the devices for building credibility.

Appealing to Audience Motives and Emotions

Kenneth Burke, a noted rhetorical critic, observed that "you persuade a man only insofar as you talk his language by speech, gesture, tonality, order, image, attitude, idea, *identifying* your ways with his." [19] The four devices for building your credibility, discussed in the previous section, provide one orientation toward accomplishing this persuasive task. Involving your audience in the persuasive act through *motivational* and *emotional* appeals is another orientation. Using this approach, a speaker seeks to identify the cause or proposal advanced with the needs, desires, and wishes of the audience being addressed.

Motives are generalized states that we seek to satisfy or that we seek to have satisfied by others. Brembeck and Howell[20] classified motives into two broad categories: physiological—hunger, thirst, rest; and socio-psychological—friendship, self-esteem, social approval, achievement. Over two thousand years ago, Aristotle observed that people are motivated by the following goals:

Happiness	Magnificence	Honor
Justice	Health	Reputation
Courage	Beauty	Power
Temperance	Wealth	Knowledge
Magnanimity	Friendship	Life[21]

More recently, Bette G. Blackburn noted that people fear or are motivated to avoid the following events:

Loss of national security, nuclear war, loss of democracy
The power of a Supreme Being, fate after death
Loss of, or harm to, loved ones
Lack of success in job or profession
Loss of life or health
Social disapproval
Poor or incomplete family life
Loss of mind or of emotional control
Lack of money, or financial hardship
Loss of status in the community
Being caught doing wrong
Losing, or being unable to make, friends
Failure
Inability to raise children properly
Inability to establish meaningful love relationships
Being unknowingly influenced by others
Harming others[22]

While scholars may differ in the motives they choose to emphasize, few would claim that motives lack significance as determinants of human behavior.

Human *emotions* are more generalized affective states that may move us toward the satisfaction of a physiological or socio-psychological need. Among the emotions which may be identified are delight, joy, elation, hope, gratitude, affection, love, shame, anger, hate, fear, envy, sorrow, grief, anxiety, sympathy, and pity.

Appeals to motives and emotions are frequently combined in a persuasive message. For example, during the 1964 Presidential campaign, charges that Goldwater was an ardent militarist were accompanied by visual images of nuclear holocausts and small children cavorting in an open meadow. The images, when juxtaposed, called forth the emotions of love and fear and motivated viewers to take actions that would protect children—in this case by voting against the Republican candidate. Similarly, we have all seen magazine and television advertisements picturing an emaciated child and urging a contribution to an international agency for children. In this case, our emotion (pity) is used to enlist our humanitarian motives.

As a persuader, your task is to invite the participation of the audience by addressing their basic emotions and motives. Once you have selected the basic emotions or motives to which you wish to appeal, you need only provide supporting materials (often specific instances) and vivid language to trigger the desired response. In his speech to the Inland Daily Press Association, Jenkin Lloyd Jones appealed to a variety of audience emotions and motives using a variety of supporting materials and emotionally-charged language. In support of his contention that American entertainment is in a sorry state he noted:

> Can anyone deny that movies are dirtier than ever? But they don't call it dirt. They call it "realism." Why do we let them fool us? Why do we nod owlishly when they tell us that filth is merely a daring art form, that licentiousness is really social comment? Isn't it time we recognized Hollywood's quest for the fast buck for what it is? Isn't it plain that the financially-harassed movie industry is putting gobs of sex in the darkened drive-ins in an effort to lure curious teenagers away from their TV sets? Last week the screen industry solemnly announced that henceforth perversion and homosexuality would no longer be barred from the screen provided the subjects were handled with "delicacy and taste." Good Lord!
>
> And we of the press are a party to the crime. Last year the movie ads in our newspaper got so salacious and suggestive that the advertising manager and I decided to throw out the worst and set up some standards. We thought that due to our ukase there might be some interruption in advertising some shows. But no. Within a couple of hours the exhibitors were down with much milder ads. How was this miracle accomplished?
>
> Well, it seems that the exhibitors are supplied with several different ads for each movie. If the publishers are dumb enough to accept the most suggestive ones, those are what they get. But if publishers squawk, the cleaner ads are sent down. Isn't it time we all squawked?
>
> I think it's time we quit giving page 1 play to the extramarital junkets of crooners. I think it is time we stopped treating as glamorous and exciting the brazen shack-ups of screen tramps. I think it is time we asked our Broadway and Hollywood columnists if they can't find something decent and inspiring going on along their beats.

> And the stage: They raided Minsky's so Minsky's has spread all over town. Bawdiness has put on a dinner jacket, and seats in the orchestra that used to go for six-bits at the Old Howard and Nichols' Gayety are now at $8.80. Oh, yes. And we have lots of "realism." Incestuous Americans. Perverted Americans. Degenerate Americans. Murderous Americans.
>
> How many of these "realistic" Americans do you know?
>
> Two months ago an American touring company, sponsored by the State Department and paid for by our tax dollars, presented one of Tennessee Williams' more depraved offerings to an audience in Rio de Janeiro. The audience hooted in disgust and walked out. And where did it walk to? Right across the street where a Russian ballet company was putting on a beautiful performance for the glory of Russia! How dumb can we get?
>
> We are drowning our youngsters in violence, cynicism and sadism piped into the living room and even the nursery. The grandchildren of the kids who used to weep because The Little Match Girl froze to death now feel cheated if she isn't slugged, raped, and thrown into a Bessemer converter.[23]

While you may not agree with the positions taken by Jones, it is hard to imagine that members of his audience looked on in dispassionate aloofness. If an audience is to make the speaker's cause their own, they must come to feel a strong emotional attachment to the proposition being advocated.

EXERCISES

VERIFICATION

20. Identify three motives and three emotions mentioned in the text.

VERIFICATION

21. Identify one of the three descriptions below as "emotions" and another as "motives."

a. ____________________ appeals to the audience's willingness to act as the speaker wishes

b. ____________________ generalized states that people seek to satisfy

c. ____________________ affective states that can be appealed to in obtaining appropriate response

UTILIZATION

22. Identify the following descriptions of commercials as they employ either an appeal to emotion or to motive.

a. ____________________ A tear runs down the cheek of an American Indian as he sees rubbish thrown from a passing automobile.

b. ____________________ A dumpy looking young woman is walking along the beach in an unattractive dress. The camera fades and she emerges as a trim young woman in a bikini. Her labored walk becomes a graceful jog.

c. ____________________ Earthquake victims are pictured with cups in hand, waiting in a long line for their gruel.

d. ____________________ A shifty looking character is pictured stuffing objects from a store counter into his baggy pockets. The superimposed words read, "Shoplifters take everybody's money."

UTILIZATION

23. Analyze the use of specific appeals to motives and emotions in the sample speech presented below.

Our Indian people are careful with their money. For example, our Indian people voted to have their profit sharing put back for retirement. They voted to do this for one main reason—they don't want to be dependent upon anyone else again; they want to stand on their own two feet. All the Indian people are asking for is a chance. They've had it up to here with handouts—they don't want that. They only want you to respect them for what they are as human beings, and to give them an opportunity. If we look to Washington to solve this problem, there will be many generations doing so. I think as American citizens, as business people, we can solve this problem much faster. We now have 171 plants employing 12,500 people in Indian areas, but this is not nearly enough. We need much more.

I don't know what you want out of life. Maybe you want to be as rich as J. Paul Getty. That's not too big a goal, but it really won't mean much to you in terms of happiness and quality of life. Maybe you want to be big, important and respected. That's a pretty good goal. I think we all should have that in mind. But when you boil it all down, wouldn't you just like to know that you gave another fellow human being a chance at a better quality of life? That's a far better goal and it's one that you can easily attain.[24]

UTILIZATION

24. Create a one to two minute speech appealing to a basic motive or emotion using emotionally charged specific instances and vivid language.

Preparing Your Persuasive Speech

In this book, you have been introduced to a wide array of information useful in preparing a persuasive speech. The purpose of this section is to guide your efforts as you seek a synthesis of these diverse elements. We will begin this section by suggesting the way in which attempts to use evidence, build credibility, and appeal to audience motives and emotions, may all be brought together in affirming your major contentions. We will then present a persuasive speech evaluation form to identify the broad range of factors that you must consider in preparing your persuasive speech and in criticizing the persuasive speeches of others. Finally, we will provide two sample persuasive speeches to test your understanding of the principles of persuasive speaking in action.

Blending the Persuasive Elements

As you amass evidence, in the form of testimony, specific instances, and statistics, you need to think about how you can use the material to maximize audience interest and involvement in your message. The "power" of a persuasive message comes not only through the presentation of raw data but also through the marshalling of your evidence, your credibility, and your appeals to audience motives and emotions to substantiate a point.

To demonstrate how the persuasive elements may blend in giving credence to an idea, let us return to our old friend "The Abominable Snowman." One of our supporting contentions was that "people have seen the creature." Consider how you might use a variety of persuasive elements to secure audience belief.

Statement of First Contention	I realize that I invite your skepticism when I tell you that *people have seen the Abominable Snowman.*
Credibility: Good Will toward the Audience	You are intelligent people who have been taught, and justly so, to withhold belief until the weight of evidence compels your acceptance.
Credibility: Qualifications	As a science major, I too have learned the value of skepticism; the consequences of arriving at a premature conclusion are often severe and sometimes fatal.
Credibility: Desirable Personal Qualities	Still, I have also been taught to have an open mind; it is equally dangerous to reject an idea because it is unpopular. And so, when I began my research in Tall Peak, Colorado—alleged home of "the snowman" —it was in the spirit of dispassionate inquiry.
Evidence: Specific Instances	Consider with me what I learned. I began my research by examining the official ledger of the sheriff of Mountain County. Sept. 27, 1977: 4:00 p.m. Tall Peak Scout Troop 27 reports encounter with tall, shaggy white creature in Rugged Canyon. Tenderfoot Scout faints. Sept. 29, 1977: 7:57 p.m. Eight-foot beast sighted by skinny-dippers at Miller's Pond. Oct. 1, 1977: 5:47 a.m. Visual identification of large white creature made by members of The Early Bird, Bird Watchers Club at Forest Hills Sanctuary. The ledger proceeds for three more pages. Do you sense a pattern?
Evidence: Statistics	A poll of citizens of Mountain County, conducted by Random Samples, Incorporated, disclosed that forty-five citizens, 90 percent of those surveyed, reported seeing a tall, white, shaggy man-like beast within the past three years.

Evidence: Testimony	Do you need more evidence? While talking to people in Tall Peak I met I. M. Cautious, Professor of Mountain Phenomenology at Colorado State Institute, who noted: "I came here to talk with people who had seen the creature. Imagine my surprise when I almost ran him (her) over at the intersection of Bluff Road and Gurgling Creek Trail. Let me tell you—the Abominable Snowman exists. Of this there can be no doubt. I'm a scientist and I have seen him (her)." Have people seen the Abominable Snowman?
Appeal to Audience Motives and Emotions: Rationality	What do you think? The evidence overwhelmingly supports the fact that a creature has been seen, and that creature is neither human nor of an animal species that you or I can label or identify. Reason tells us that this amazing array of evidence may not be explained by chance, local insanity, or a conspiracy. A strange creature *has* been seen.

Although this hypothetical example is an exercise in creative writing, rather than honest advocacy, it does suggest that the elements of evidence, speaker credibility, and audience appeal may be blended to render a line of argument appealing to an audience. It remains for you to demonstrate that this kind of synthesis can be accomplished while using real evidence, real credibility appeals, and real appeals to audience motives and emotions.

Persuasive Speech Evaluation Form

Introduction *Comments*

Statement to Focus Attention
Statement to Enhance Credibility
Statement of Importance
Statements Providing Background
Proposition (Identify):
Statement of Partition

Body

Contentions (Identify and Evaluate):

Types of Evidence Used (Identify and Evaluate):

Appeals to Motives and Emotions (Identify and Evaluate):

Attempts to Build Credibility (Identify and Evaluate):

Conclusion

Devices Used:

Effectiveness:

Transitions (Identify and Evaluate):

Language Usage

Clarity

Appropriateness

Vividness

Delivery

Physical Aspects

Vocal Aspects

Overall Persuasive Effect

Sex Education in the Schools

Dean Brasser

1. I'd like to speak to you today on sex education in the public schools. A few weeks ago, we were asked to express our views on a variety of current topics. At that time, everyone in our class indicated that they were in favor of sex education in the public schools. So I thought it would be a good idea to use all of the methods we learned in class and, to quote the Com Arts 105 Schedule of Assignments, present, "A five-minute speech demonstrating excellence in the use of logical and emotional proofs," and I wanted to prove that sex education was wrong and dangerous.

2. With this plan in mind, I proceeded to the periodical room of the Memorial Library, drew up a long list of possible sources, and lost myself somewhere up in the stacks. But when I left the stacks, I had a different plan in mind. After searching for hours, trying to find a logical argument against public-school sex education, I was forced to conclude that there simply was none.

3. The most vocal opponents to public-school sex education today are the John Birch Society's Movement to Restore Decency to Education, the American Education Lobby, and an organization called MOMS, which is short for Mothers Organized for Moral Stability. There are three basic arguments used by these groups. First, that there really is no need for sex education; second, that increased exposure to sex topics would merely lead to increased sex play among teenagers; and third, that even if there is a need, sex education should be handled in the home and in the church, not in the schools.

4. Today I would like to help you see how wrong these arguments really are.

5. The first contention of the sex education opponents is that, "There really is no need for sex education programs at all," and their reasoning: they never had sex education classes in school and they turned out all right. Can't these people see what's happening around them? Venereal disease is the number two communicable disease in the United States, second only to the common cold, yet one-third of the students surveyed this fall by the University of Wisconsin Health Center did not know how to find out if they actually had the disease even if they already suspected it. Lee Rainwater and Karol Weinstein, authors of *And the Poor Get Children,* found a strong correlation between unwed motherhood and superstition concerning the dangers of contraception. Noted social psychologist John Gagnon showed evidence that preadolescent sexual misconceptions lead to deviant behavior in later life, and the United States government estimated that some 400,000 sex-related crimes were committed last year alone. It seems quite clear that, in our society, there is a great need for comprehensive sex education programs.

6. The second argument used by the crusaders for Decent Education and Moral Stability is that increased exposure in schools of sex-related topics will merely lead to increased sexual experimentation and immorality among teenagers. This argument, however, can only be speculation. The only way to judge the effects of sex education programs is through follow-up studies of actual, existing programs. Hans L. Zetterberg, chairman of the Ohio State University Department of Sociology made an extensive study of sex education in public schools in Sweden, where it has been compulsory since 1957. His findings?

> Sexual morality and customs have changed with factors such as availability of contraceptives, the emergence of the welfare state, making pregnancy less of a disaster, and the decline of organized religion among young people. Sex education has tended to follow rather than lead social trends.

Preliminary studies of several school districts in California have concurred with these results. In other words, all of the sound, scientific evidence available shows that sex education is not a cause for increased sex activity among youth as its opponents would like to believe.

7. "All right," say the anti-sex-education people, "all right, suppose there is some need for sex education, and suppose it isn't harmful;"—and here is their third point—"sex education should be handled privately in the home and in the church where it belongs and not in the public schools." Here I cannot disagree completely. Ideally, both the home and the church should provide complete sex instruction, leaving the schools free to concentrate in other areas. But the problem lies in the fact that homes and churches have not provided decent sex education in the past, and there is no reason to expect them to do so in the future. In 1970, a study of this problem by H. D. Thornburg, Doctor of Education and Assistant Professor of Educational Psychology at the University of Arizona, revealed that, of the college students surveyed, only one-fourth had received any real sex education at home, only one percent had received sex information from their church or physician, and that there is legitimate concern as to the amount of, as well as the accuracy of, sex information among our youth. Lester A. Kirkendall, a respected psychologist, summed up the situation quite well in an interview for *Reader's Digest:*

> There are limits to what even the best intentioned parents can do. As children begin to reach outside the home for relationships, they stop talking about sex, and by the teen years most young people are too embarrassed to ask questions. Thus, somebody else has to do the job, and the schools are the logical choice. After all, their function is to educate.

8. Surely we can see that sex education is greatly needed in this society, and the institutions with the best possible chance of carrying out such programs are the public schools.

9. Public-school sex-education programs have received the full support of the National Education Association, the United States Department of Health, Education, and Welfare, and the American Medical Association; yet there are still organizations and individuals who persist in condemning such programs. These reactionary elements have labeled public-school sex education as "perversion," "raw sex in the classrooms," and, here it comes, "a Communist conspiracy to corrupt American youth." When will these people come to their senses and admit that sex education is desperately needed, and in the public schools where all can benefit? For the sake of future generations, we can only hope that this realization comes very soon.[25]

Is Busing The Answer?

by

John L. Kitslaar

1. Busing—a word that can silence a room full of people as neatly as a pistol shot—a word that vividly recreates images of parents picketing and

children traveling to school with police escorts—a word that divides communities.

2. When people talk about busing, they're talking about court-ordered or forced busing of students. Ostensibly undertaken to desegregate schools and thus improve their racial balance, forced busing means that blacks are physically transported to predominantly white schools, and vice versa. It is a "tool" that has become ever more popular with the courts, and it is a "tool" that has been met by hostile reaction and turmoil in many of our nation's communities.

3. What is the value of this program? Does it work? After carefully weighing the evidence, I have reached the conclusion that busing for the purpose of achieving desegregation should be ceased. My conclusion is based on two arguments: first, that busing does not improve the quality of education; and second, that it does not actually alter the racial balance within the schools.

4. For a long time, busing has been defended as a means of improving the quality of education received by blacks. Research shows that busing is NOT improving the quality of education. Former Secretary of Health, Education, and Welfare, Casper Weinberger, stated:

> Today most of the deliberate segregation has been dealt with, and we have fallen into a statistical approach to school desegregation.
>
> There is too much emphasis on numbers and racial balance. Often, this has no regard for education of the child or the quality of the school.

5. F. David Mathews, present Secretary of HEW and former President of the University of Alabama, concurs with Weinberger. Mathews told a Senate hearing: "It is not producing good results. I support equal educational opportunity for all children. However, any policy of the United States should be judged in terms of its effectiveness." These authorities are not alone in their judgment of busing's effectiveness. For example, a new study by Professors Levitan, Johnston, and Taggart, conducted at the George Washington University Center for Manpower Policy Studies and aptly titled, "Still a Dream," declares that school integration doesn't insure substantial improvement of black children's performance. They conclude: "the weight of the evidence seems to suggest that integration in the schools can make small improvements in black I.Q. and achievement."

6. In addition, a study by Western Michigan University Professors Schellenberg and Halteman failed to provide any evidence that elementary school children who are bussed do any better academically than those who remain in inner-city schools. There was no difference in academic achievement even though the bussed children tended to have classmates with higher achievement than classmates of those in the control group.

7. While "quality" is hard to pinpoint with accuracy, it is not hard to sympathize with the action taken by Congressman Donald Fraser. Fraser, a white and an ardent advocate of busing, enrolled his daughter in a D.C. public school—he practiced what he preached. However, when his daughter

fell behind in reading, the Frasers enrolled her in Georgetown Day, a private school. Questioned by Mike Wallace on CBS's "Sixty Minutes," Mrs. Fraser defended their action by saying "your children get educated only once." If this seems too atypical an example, consider the story of Margaret, a black junior reflecting on the "quality" achieved by busing. "I don't really have any strong feeling against busing," she said, "but my work has gone down: Not a lot, but I don't try as hard as before. It seems I don't need to. It seems like teachers at Brighton won't push you that hard and the kids won't cooperate with the teachers. So, like, spirits come down."

8. To illustrate that the lack of improvement affects whites as well, let's hear from Steve, a white senior, who states: "No, I didn't learn much. How can you study if there are police in the halls? The whole thing doesn't make any sense. Why bus kids from one shitty school to another shitty school?"

9. Yet another put-down on the wonders of integration was voiced by David Armor, a senior social scientist at the Rand Corporation, in an article based on a study of six northern cities. His conclusion: "Blacks did not attain educational gains as a result of busing programs, though such gains had been anticipated."

10. In retrospect, we have learned from the commentaries of research experts and school-age victims; without exception, they have not been positive about the value of busing as a tool to improve educational quality.

11. In addition to claiming that better quality of education will result, busing proponents also claim that the action is necessary to desegregate the schools. Busing has not achieved this laudable aim. On the contrary, it has resegregated the schools.

12. Let's look at what has happened when court ordered busing has gone into effect. In almost every instance city school enrollments have plummeted. Boston's enrollment dropped from 93,000 in 1973–74 to 72,000 in 1974–75. Now, in the spring of 1976, enrollment is at 55,000 and still dropping. Students—mostly white—have left the public schools in droves. Their departure has radically altered the racial balance within city school systems. In Atlanta, the ratio shifted from 70 percent white in 1960 to only 30 percent white in 1976. In Boston, the ratio swung from 62 percent white in 1973 to 40 percent now. Nor are these instances unusual. Englewood, California's racial balance shifted from 62 percent white in 1970 to only 19.5 percent today. School officials in Charlotte, North Carolina, estimate that 10,000 white pupils have abandoned "integrated" schools in favor of private,segregated "academies" or other school districts.

13. Conversely, as one might expect from such a white exodus, many cities now have predominantly black schools: For example:

Washington, D.C.—96 percent
Atlanta—81 percent
Chicago—58 percent

14. The shifting of black-white populations makes any plan for desegregation of the schools futile. One example will suffice: Judge Robert E. DeMascio of the federal district court in Michigan has ordered 21,200 students

in the Detroit system to be bused within Detroit, and another 7,100 to be reassigned—all for the purpose of achieving improved racial balance in the Detroit system. But 70 percent of Detroit's school enrollment is black, so how much juggling around can Judge DeMascio undertake? As Tom Turner, former Detroit NAACP chapter president, asked, in skepticism: "How many times can you put seventy into thirty?"

15. As laudable as the goals of ending racial prejudice and eliminating educational inequities are, it should be abundantly clear that busing has not—nor is it likely to—achieve any significant desegregation of the public schools.

Howard Flieger, editor of the *US News and World Report,* restates my central theme, and elaborates on its consequences:

> No reasonable person can challenge the goal of eradicating racial differences that divide Americans. But no matter how one feels about the goal of forced busing, there is no doubt that the means has inflicted hardships on children and their families; it has not ended classroom separation of the races; it has not raised the level of public education; nor has it increased voluntary integration. There must be a better way.

16. What should our attitude be as we seek this "better way?" Norman Cousins, editor of *Saturday Review* provides some advice we would do well to heed:

> There is no disgrace in having failed in an important social enterprise. The only disgrace is in persisting with failure in order to hold to commitments without regard to the need for keeping an open mind. A country dedicated to human rights should not have to confess intellectual and moral bankruptcy in attempting to provide an adequate education for all its citizens.

17. Thus, we must cultivate a willingness to unshackle ourselves from unprofitable ventures and forge ahead. Let us—through the denial of busing—renew our dedication to the goals of social justice and strive for *the better way.*[26]

EXERCISES

UTILIZATION

25. Analyze the preceding speeches using the persuasive speech evaluation form. You may omit the section on delivery. All other categories should be analyzed.

VERIFICATION

26. Prepare and deliver a four to five minute persuasive speech that meets the criteria implicit in the persuasive speech evaluation form.

Notes

1. Donald K. Smith, *Man Speaking* (New York: Dodd, Mead and Co., 1969), p. 70.

2. Winston L. Brembeck and William S. Howell, *Persuasion: A Means of Social Influence,* 2d ed. (Englewood Cliffs, N.J.: Prentice Hall, 1976), p. 19.

3. Ronee Ross, "Are Grades Really Necessary?" Unpublished Speech, University of Wisconsin, Madison, 1975.

4. Anson Mount, "The Playboy Philosophy-Pro," in Wil A. Linkugel, R. R. Allen, and Richard L. Johannesen, *Contemporary American Speeches,* 3d ed. (Belmont, Cal.: Wadsworth, 1972), p. 158.

5. James Stewart, "The Third Report and Order: The FCC Gamble That Didn't Pay Off," Unpublished Manuscript, University of Wisconsin, Madison, 1975.

6. Brent Simmons, et al., "As Time Runs Out," *Winning Orations* (1969): 76.

7. James T. Needham, "The Cost of Economic Growth," *Vital Speeches* 40, (1 October 1974): 739.

8. For a perceptive commentary on the use and abuse of statistics, see Darrell Huff, *How to Lie with Statistics* (New York: W. W. Norton, 1954).

9. Robert Hoffman, "A Plea for Improved Drug Regulation," Unpublished Manuscript, University of Wisconsin, 1976.

10. Aristotle, *Rhetoric,* translated by Rhys Roberts (New York: Modern Library, 1954), p. 25.

11. Franklin S. Haiman, "The Rhetoric of 1968: A Farewell to Rational Discourse," in Linkugel, et al., *American Speeches,* 3d ed., p. 143.

12. Douglas MacArthur, "Farewell to the Cadets," in Linkugel, et al., *American Speeches,* 3d ed., p. 287.

13. Paul Koeppe, "Let's Get the Facts on Nuclear Power," Unpublished Manuscript, University of Wisconsin, 1976.

14. David Wheatly, Unpublished Manuscript, University of Wisconsin, 1976.

15. Jenkin Lloyd Jones, "Who Is Tampering with the Soul of America?" in Linkugel, et al., *American Speeches,* 3d ed., pp. 228–29.

16. Richard M. Duesterbeck, "Man's Other Society," *Winning Orations* (1961): 101.

17. Mark Hatfield, "Noise," in Linkugel, et al., *American Speeches,* 3d ed., p. 212.

18. Mount, "Playboy Philosophy—Pro," in Linkugel, et al., *American Speeches,* 3d ed., p. 157.

19. Kenneth Burke, *A Rhetoric of Motives* (1950; rpt. Berkeley, California: University of California Press, 1969), p. 55. Copyright © 1969 by Kenneth Burke; reprinted by permission of the University of California Press.

20. Brembeck and Howell, *Persuasion,* pp. 80–124.

21. Aristotle, *Rhetoric,* pp. 92–121.

22. Bette G. Blackburn, "The Typologies of Anxiety-Arousing Areas" (M.A. Thesis, Michigan State University, 1967) quoted in James C. McCroskey, *An Introduction to Rhetorical Communication* (Englewood Cliffs, N.J.: Prentice-Hall, Inc., 1968), p. 129.

23. Jones, "Soul of America?" in Linkugel, et al., *American Speeches,* 3d ed., pp. 226–27.

24. Donald Greve, "The American Indian," *Vital Speeches* 36 (15 February 1970): 278–79.

25. Dean Brasser, "Sex Education in the Schools," Unpublished Manuscript, University of Wisconsin, 1972.

26. John L. Kitslaar, "Is Busing the Answer?" Unpublished Manuscript, University of Wisconsin, 1976.

7

ceremonial speaking

learning objectives

By the conclusion of this chapter you will be able to:

1. Identify ten types of ceremonial speeches
2. Match definitions of ceremonial genre with speech type
3. Identify speech fragments according to the genre of ceremonial discourse in which they occur
4. Analyze the appropriateness of specimen ceremonial speeches
5. Construct a list of topics appropriate to a particular subject, audience, and ceremonial occasion
6. Identify six guidelines for ceremonial speaking
7. Match guidelines with brief descriptions
8. Identify the guidelines that are violated in specimen descriptions of rhetorical events
9. Analyze sample speeches against the criteria implicit in the six guidelines for ceremonial speaking.
10. Prepare and deliver a ceremonial speech that matches the criteria implicit in the six guidelines for ceremonial speaking.

> Epidictic discourse sets out to increase the intensity of adherence to certain values, which might not be contested when considered on their own but may nevertheless not prevail against other values that might come into conflict with them. The speaker tries to establish a sense of communion centered around particular values recognized by the audience, and to this end . . . uses the whole range of means available to the rhetorician for purposes of amplification and enhancement.[1]
>
> Perelman

Perelman, in the headnote to this chapter, identified the central role that values play in ceremonial (epidictic) discourse. When people come together to pay honor to outstanding members of their profession, or to eulogize the dead, or to recognize the accomplishments of a graduating class, they expect that the speeches given will serve the ceremonial function that has brought them together. By appealing to values that are cherished by those assembled, the speaker attempts to create a sense of communion within the audience.

As you read the pages of this chapter, you will be reminded of the importance of such speeches in contemporary life. Section one considers the wide array of ceremonial speeches. Section two identifies the rhetorical means through which compelling reexpression is given to cherished values. The final section presents sample speeches for your analysis.

The Genre of Ceremonial Speaking

There are many ceremonial events that require appropriate words: political victories must be observed; important events in history must be commemorated; new buildings must be dedicated; seniors must be formally graduated; and awards must be given. In all societies, throughout all times, public ceremonies have been held to mark important social moments and to inspire rededication to social values.

The speeches given in such public ceremonies are restricted by the ceremonial purpose of the gathering. The college professor who devotes his or her commencement speech to an explanation of medieval architecture and the mayor who argues for urban renewal at the dedication ceremony for a new arts center have both failed in their analysis of the rhetorical situation. Audience expectations have not been met; the ceremonial function has not been served. Perelman cautioned against such faulty analysis when he observed:

> It is because epidictic discourse is intended to promote values on which there is agreement that one has an impression of misuse when in a speech of this kind someone takes up a position on a controversial question, turns the argument toward disputed values, and introduces a discordant note on an occasion that is liable to promote communion. . . .[2]

As there is a time for imparting knowledge and a time for advocating a controversial position, there is also a time for inspiring a recommitment to social values. In this section, we will consider ten types of speeches that promote values while satisfying ceremonial functions.

Acceptance Speeches

It is the rare organization that does not, at some moment, present an award, an honor, or a gift to a member of that organization. Why do media artists give Oscars, Emmys, and Grammys to outstanding members of their profession? Why do college sports programs sponsor award banquets? Why do companies publicly present bejeweled pins and watches to longtime employees? Why do teachers' organizations select and honor a "teacher of the year"? We honor others because they symbolize the values of members of our group.

When you are chosen for such an "honor," as surely you will be, your rhetorical "moves" are strongly dictated by audience expectations. You are expected to be appreciative—"This is the greatest moment of my life." You are expected to be humble—"Gee Whiz, I couldn't have done it without the help of the coach and those wonderful gals who fed me the ball." You are expected to be dedicated—"Since I was a boy I have wanted to be the county's best chicken plucker; it has been my life and my love." Your goal is to project the personal qualities that the award is meant to honor.

Must you be trite, vacuous, and inane to achieve this ceremonial function? Decidedly not! Consider the opening words of General MacArthur as he rose to accept the Sylvanus Thayer award for service to his nation:

> No human being could fail to be deeply moved by such a tribute as this, coming from a profession I have served so long and a people I have loved so well.
>
> It fills me with an emotion I cannot express. But this award is not intended primarily to honor a personality, but to symbolize a great moral code—the code of conduct and chivalry of those who guard this beloved land of culture and ancient descent. That is the animation of this medallion. For all eyes and for all time it is an expression of the ethics of the American soldier. That I should be integrated in this way with

> so noble an ideal arouses a sense of pride and yet of humility, which will be with me always.
>
> Duty, honor, country: those three hallowed words reverently dictate what you want to be, what you can be, what you will be. They are your rallying points to build courage when courage seems to fail, to regain faith when there seems to be little cause for faith, to create hope when hope becomes forlorn.[3]

In the long speech that followed, MacArthur inspired recommitment to the values of duty, honor, and country in the professional life of the American soldier.

Commencement Speeches

Do you remember your high school commencement ceremony? Of course you do. But do you remember the main speaker at your high school commencement ceremony? Most people don't. But what did he or she say? Do you remember? If he or she behaved in predictable ways, your speaker probably began by noting sacrifices you and your parents made to get you to that moment. Your speaker in all probability then referred to the nature of the world that you were about to enter. (It was a grim world, wasn't it?) Then your commencement speaker held out hope for the contributions you and your classmates would make to the resolution of world problems.

During the protest years, high school and college student commencement speakers faced a dilemma. They knew that they were expected to praise the achievement of the graduating class and project hope for the world they were about to enter. However, they could not in good conscience utter "social niceties" in the face of "massive social injustice." Consequently, they chose to indict the establishment. They attacked a nation engaged in a senseless and brutal war, a social system that demonstrated discrimination against ethnic and social minorities, and an educational system that seemed arbitrary, vindictive, and irrelevant. Such student speakers, predictably, were little acclaimed by the parents, faculty members, and representatives of the general public who were assembled for those commencements.

Must a successful commencement speaker sacrifice intellectual integrity at the altar of rhetoric? We believe not. In March 1954, Adlai Stevenson, in a speech prepared for the Senior Class Banquet at Princeton University, began by observing:

> I am informed that this senior class banquet is being held at the expense of your accumulated reserves. I suggest that inviting me here

> is a very perilous thing to do because certainly within a few hours the Republicans will ask for equivalent time.
>
> I was delighted to witness a moment ago your emphatic approval of my program for Princeton some thirty-two years ago—unlimited cuts, non-compulsory Chapel, and student firing of the Dean. I always considered that it was wise in politics to have—shall we say—a popular program. The trouble is that when I went into politics it appears that I changed my views.
>
> I feel as though I were opening the hunting season on college seniors. From now until mid-June, college seniors are fair game for all of us uplifters, viewers with alarm, Chautauqua-style orators, even for occasional unemployed politicians. From now until mid-June, college seniors are to be repeatedly reminded how fortunate they are and what they should do with their hard-won educational disciplines; they are to be warned repeatedly that the old order is changing, that the sky is overcast, visibility is low; and they are to be urged and goaded and implored to accept the challenge to remake the future.
>
> . . . if I cannot advise you on how to solve the momentous problems of your future, perhaps I can venture to suggest some duties and, if you please, some rules of conduct that, it seems to me, devolve upon the educated man. I would speak, then, about the educated man and his government, and about the educated man and his university.[4]

In the minutes that followed, Stevenson gave impelling reexpression to the values of responsible citizenship, as they relate to one's nation and one's university. Although dealing with old values, he made them come alive through his fresh use of language and his judicious use of supporting materials. He met the ceremonial requirements of the gathering without sacrificing his integrity as an intellectual and as a human being.

Commemorative Speeches

Commemorative speeches acknowledge the occurrence of significant social events. In 1976, thousands of public ceremonies commemorated the 200th anniversary of the founding of our nation. Each year groups of Americans commemorate such diverse events as the birth of Abraham Lincoln, the conclusion of World War I, the passage of the twenty-first amendment, the attack of the Japanese on Pearl Harbor, and the assassination of President Kennedy. Such speeches usually describe the event in question and ponder its relevance to contemporary life.

The power of this speech genre was demonstrated by President Kennedy when, on June 26, 1963, he commemorated the eighteenth anniversary of the dramatic physical separation of West Berlin from the remainder of the free world. In a speech punctuated by clapping, crying, and cheering by the impassioned mass assembled, Kennedy observed:

> I am proud to come to this city as the guest of your distinguished Mayor, who has symbolized throughout the world the fighting spirit of West Berlin. And I am proud to visit the Federal Republic with your distinguished Chancellor who for so many years has committed Germany to democracy and freedom and progress, and to come here in the company of my fellow American, General Clay, who has been in this city during its great moments of crisis and will come again if ever needed.
>
> Two thousand years ago the proudest boast was *"civis Romanus sum."* Today, in the world of freedom, the proudest boast is *"Ich bin ein Berliner."*
>
> I appreciate my interpreter translating my German!
>
> There are many people in the world who really don't understand, or say they don't, what is the great issue between the free world and the Communist world. Let them come to Berlin. There are some who say that Communism is the wave of the future. Let them come to Berlin. And there are some who say in Europe and elsewhere we can work with the Communists. Let them come to Berlin. And there are even a few who say that it is true that Communism is an evil system, but it permits us to make economic progress. *Lass' sie nach Berlin kommen.* Let them come to Berlin.
>
> Freedom has many difficulties and democracy is not perfect, but we have never had to put a wall up to keep our people in, to prevent them from leaving us. I want to say, on behalf of my countrymen, who live many miles away on the other side of the Atlantic, who are far distant from you, that they take the greatest pride that they have been able to share with you, even from a distance, the story of the last eighteen years. I know of no town, no city, that has been besieged for 18 years that still lives with the vitality and the force, and the hope and the determination of the city of West Berlin. While the wall is the most obvious and vivid demonstration of the failures of the Communist system, for all the world to see, we take no satisfaction in it, for it is, as your Mayor has said, an offense not only against history but an offense against humanity, separating families, dividing husbands and wives and brothers and sisters, and dividing a people who wish to be joined together.[5]

In commemorating a sad moment of recent history, Kennedy valued democracy, freedom, vitality, hope, and determination while deprecating Communism, oppression, and inhumanity.

Dedication Speeches

America is a nation of builders. As each edifice is completed, we gather to pay tribute. We honor the completion of such diverse structures as highways, bridges, school buildings, office complexes, shopping centers, public swimming pools, libraries, art centers, books, and bicycle trails. At such moments, following the cutting of the ceremonial ribbon, a speech of dedication is usually given.

By tradition, the speech of dedication pays tribute to the sacrifices that enabled the completion of the task and to the value of the product to the lives of those assembled. Recently, the authors attended a dedication ceremony for a new communication arts building on a university campus. The speakers included the university chancellor, a state senator, a dean, and the chairman of the department. Although the speakers approached the dedication ceremony from different perspectives, each speaker addressed the same basic themes. Each speaker paid tribute to the persons who unselfishly fought for the dream encapsulated by the new building (the people differed but the "dream" was the same). Each speaker spoke about the value of the structure to the life of the community it was to serve: the chancellor spoke of the role of the structure in the life of the university community; the state senator valued the building as a cultural center for the city and county; the dean praised the building as a setting for college teaching, research, and community service; and the chairman spoke of the role of the building in the life of his department.

Eulogies

Eulogies are speeches that pay tribute to the lives of individuals. They are most frequently given as part of memorial services. They may honor a single person, as in a funeral service, or a collection of persons, as in Memorial Day services. By tradition, such speeches mourn the passing of the person being honored and find, in the life of the departed, values that may give strength and rededication to those who remain. However, eulogies may also be used to praise the living.

When in June 1968 Robert F. Kennedy was assassinated, Senator Edward M. Kennedy was appointed to deliver the eulogy to his brother's memory. Speaking in a voice at times choked by emotion, he said:

> Your eminences, your excellencies, Mr. President. In behalf of Mrs. Kennedy, her children, the parents and sisters of Robert Kennedy, I want to express what we feel to those who mourn with us today in this cathedral and around the world.

> We loved him as a brother and as a father and as a son. From his parents and from his older brothers and sisters, Joe and Kathleen and Jack, he received an inspiration which he passed on to all of us.
>
> He gave us strength in time of trouble, wisdom in time of uncertainty, and sharing in time of unhappiness. He will always be by our side.
>
> Love is not an easy feeling to put in words. Nor is loyalty or trust or joy. But he was all of these. He loved life completely, and he lived it intensely.[6]

In the minutes that followed, Senator Kennedy sought to capture the spirit of his deceased brother by quoting extensively from the words of Robert Kennedy. He concluded with a quotation that characterized the essence of Robert Kennedy—"Some men see things as they are and say 'Why?' I dream things that never were and say, 'Why not?'"

When the eulogy is given as part of a funeral service, the speaker must be especially sensitive to the grief being experienced by those who knew and loved the deceased. It is inappropriate on such occasions to allude to facets of the deceased's character that are less than noble. With the passage of time, in settings unencumbered by the funeral bier, one may present a more balanced and human portrayal of the values reflected in the life of the deceased.

Farewell Speeches

There was a time in American history when a person was born, schooled, employed, and buried in the same community. That time is over. Americans are now moving across country with almost the same ease as they once moved across town. One of the consequences of this mobility is the frequency with which people must say goodbye to groups of people with whom they have been associated. When a member must leave a group, a luncheon or other public ceremony is often scheduled to wish the departing member a formal farewell. As a part of that ceremony, the departing member is often expected to give a farewell speech.

Although farewell speeches differ substantially in emotional temper, seriousness, and length, most speeches of this type comment on the quality of the experiences shared with the group and describe the emotions that the speaker experiences as he or she leaves that group. On February 11, 1861, Abraham Lincoln delivered a farewell speech from the rear of a train as he prepared to leave Springfield, Illinois to take up the duties of the presidency. In this speech, he spoke of both the quality of his life in Springfield and his feelings as he began a new life when he said:

> My friends:
>
> No one, not in my situation, can appreciate my feeling of sadness at this parting. To this place, and the kindness of these people, I owe everything. Here I have lived a quarter of a century, and have passed from a young to an old man. Here my children have been born, and one is buried. I now leave, not knowing when or whether ever I may return, with a task before me greater than that which rested upon Washington. Without the assistance of that Divine Being who ever attended him, I cannot succeed. With that assistance, I cannot fail. Trusting in Him who can go with me, and remain with you, and be everywhere for good, let us confidently hope that all will yet be well. To His care commending you, as I hope in your prayers you will commend me, I bid you an affectionate farewell.[7]

It is reported that both Lincoln and his audience were deeply moved by the occasion. As you depart from a group, the farewell address permits you to leave some small part of yourself behind. Since your parting is the central cause for the ceremony, it is important that you choose your words wisely.

Inaugural Addresses

Almost all organizations periodically elect new leadership. When the new group president or chairperson assumes his or her office, it is often expected that the new leader will present an inaugural address symbolizing the transfer of leadership.

Among the best-known inaugural addresses are those given every four years by the incoming or reelected president of the United States. In chapter three, you studied one of the most memorable of recent presidential inaugural addresses. In that speech, President Kennedy set forth the tone and temper of his new administration in such memorable phrases as:

> Let the word go forth from this time and place, to friend and foe alike, that the torch has been passed to a new generation of Americans. . . .
>
> If a free society cannot help the many who are poor, it cannot save the few who are rich. . . .
>
> Let us never negotiate out of fear. But let us never fear to negotiate. . . .
>
> And so my fellow Americans: Ask not what your country can do for you—ask what you can do for your country. My fellow citizens of the world: ask not what America will do for you, but what together we can do for the freedom of man.[8]

The presidential inaugural address seldom sets forth specific lines of policy. Rather, as in this case, it seeks to unite the country following a period of partisan rivalry by reaffirming commitment to significant group values.

When the gavel is next passed to you, (a) note the passage of leadership, (b) praise past group values and achievements, and (c) identify the challenges that you perceive for the future. A well-presented inaugural address can convince the audience of its wisdom in choosing you and can rekindle commitment to the values and goals of the organization.

Keynote Speeches

Many conventions and meetings begin with a speech intended to highlight the importance of group deliberations. These addresses, called keynote speeches, are intended to make the listeners feel that their presence is important and that the meeting is worthwhile.

The best-known keynote speeches are those that are given every four years at the beginning of the Presidential Nominating Convention of the Democratic and Republican parties. Through the use of vivid language and strong emotional appeals, the political convention keynoter seeks to inspire enthusiasm for the significant task of choosing the next President of the United States.

While most keynote speeches are given in less dramatic circumstances, their purpose remains the same. Consider, for example, the closing paragraphs of a keynote address delivered by Joseph T. Ling, vice-president of the 3M Company, at the opening of the Convention of the American Water Works Association in Minneapolis, Minnesota, on June 9, 1975:

> If I can contribute anything as I stand here at the start of your program today, it is to urge each of you as experts in the field—and as members of the AWWA—to participate in the formulation of forthcoming water research and development activities, whether on a federal, state, or local basis. You will, for example, have an opportunity to make recommendations and to comment on the National Academy of Science report that will be used in establishing Revised National Primary Drinking Water Regulations.
>
> It is very important for us as technical members of the water utility industry to help in interpreting various research data in our field to assure that the information is not overly massaged.
>
> Your counsel on such matters is important and it is needed—individually and as a group—to assist legislators—such as Senator Humphrey, administrators and others engaged in drafting or commenting on water research policy. Only in this way are the available research and de-

velopment funds likely to be devoted to the most critical needs in a coordinated and well directed manner.

Information developed through today's research efforts will determine tomorrow's national water policy. This policy will have a profound effect on the lifestyles and values of future generations, so the task in front of us is a critical one. In Chinese writing, the word "crisis" is pronounced as "Wei-jee." In direct translation, "Wei-jee" means crisis creates opportunity. I hope all of us in the water industry take advantage of this opportunity.

With, and only with your help, can our national water research be the key to quality service in the 1980s—and beyond.[9]

Mr. Ling made each member of the AWWA convention feel that he or she had something to contribute. Furthermore, he inspired commitment to the convention undertakings by noting the critical nature of the topic under consideration. Such is the purpose of the keynote speech.

Presentation Speeches

Earlier in this section the nature of the acceptance speech was considered. The speech which precedes the acceptance speech, and which pays tribute to the man or woman being honored, is called the presentation speech. The presentation speech is designed to accomplish two functions: (a) it must clarify the nature of the award and the qualities which it is intended to honor, and (b) it must discuss the qualities of the person chosen that make the award appropriate in this particular instance.

Even the President of the United States does not escape the duty of presenting awards. On March 28, 1951, Harry S. Truman presented an award to President Auriol of France at a State Dinner.

I have a pleasant duty to perform in presenting you with this decoration. We know that you deserve it, and we hope you will wear it with pleasure.

[Reading citation] "The President of the United States of America, authorized by Act of Congress July 20, 1942, has awarded the Legion of Merit, Degree of Chief-Commander, to His Excellency Vincent Auriol, President of the French Republic and Commander in Chief of her armed forces, for exceptionally meritorious conduct in the performance of outstanding service.

His Excellency, Vincent Auriol, President of the French Republic, and Commander in Chief of her armed forces since January 1947, has displayed unswerving friendship to the United States and to the ideals

> held by all democratic nations, and has done much to assure the success of these ideals. His constant aim in stimulating the historical bonds of close friendship between France and the United States, and his strong backing of a mutual, progressive, and liberal foreign policy, have presented the rest of the world with the guiding example of continuing cooperation between the Republic of France and the United States of America." Signed by the President, and dated at the White House.
>
> I drink a toast to His Excellency, the President of France, to the first official visit that any President of France has ever paid to the United States.[10]

Although this presentation speech is wrapped in the language of protocol, it does reveal the two essential ingredients of a presentation speech: the nature of the award, and the qualities of the person chosen for the award.

Welcoming Speeches

There are numerous occasions when social organizations express welcome to visitors or new members of the organization: college presidents welcome freshman; business executives welcome foreign businessmen; and leaders of clubs extend welcomes to new members.

Although the speech of welcome occurs in diverse social settings, it normally consists of two essential parts: a statement of greeting, and a statement that relates the values of the group extending the greeting to the values of the person or persons to whom the welcome is extended. The requirements of this genre were illustrated by President Truman when he extended the nation's welcome to the President of Ecuador on June 20, 1951. He observed:

> Mr. President: It is a great pleasure to welcome you to the United States. We shall do all in our power to make your stay among us pleasant and interesting.
>
> I am pleased to extend this welcome to you. . . . We share with you a common devotion to the democratic way of life. Your visit is a symbol of the longstanding friendship that has always existed between our two countries.
>
> It is a source of gratification that Ecuador and the United States are working together with the other free nations to assure the security and peace of the world. Our countries are inspired by a high regard for individual freedom and human welfare.
>
> We are honored by your visit and most heartily extend our best wishes to you personally for the prosperity and well-being of the people of your great country. Mr. President, you are most welcome.[11]

In this section, we have considered ten types of ceremonial speeches. When effectively done, such speeches play an important role in fostering rededication to group values and in providing pleasure from public ceremony.

EXERCISES

VERIFICATION

1. Identify the ten types of ceremonial speeches.

VERIFICATION

2. Match the definitions of ceremonial speeches with the names of the types. (Caution: One of the definitions does not apply.)

a. ____________ Appropriate when leaving office

b. ____________ Highlights the theme or purpose of a conference

c. ____________ Acknowledges receipt of an award

d. ____________ Honors the dreams of those who made a project possible

e. ____________ A speech of greeting

f. ____________ Honors the completion of a degree program

g. ____________ Honors the dead

h. ____________ Acknowledges the significance of a social or historical event

i. ____________ Presents needed information

j. ____________ Symbolizes transfer of leadership

k. ____________ Honors the accomplishment of a person

UTILIZATION

3. Identify the following speech fragments according to the type of ceremonial speech in which they occur.

a. ____________________ On this, the occasion of my first day in office, I take pride in citing the accomplishments of my predecessor. Still, there is much to be done if we wish our organization to grow and prosper.

b. ____________________ We pray that those who pass through these portals will recall the energies of those who made this museum possible.

c. ____________________ Mr. Lockjaw, on behalf of my fellow club members, it is my pleasure to award you the "Speaker of the Year" trophy.

d. ____________________ For those who remain, the sense of loss must be supplanted by the example she set. We must forever strive to live as she lived. Her honesty and courage in the face of a terminal illness sets an example for all of us.

e. ____________________ I am honored by your recognition of my accomplishments, but I must accept this on behalf of all my loyal teammates. They provided the holes. I just carried the ball.

f. ____________________ I cannot offer you answers to the mysteries of life. I cannot offer you solutions to the problems you will face. But this much I can and do offer you—my sincere best wishes as you embark on yet another journey through life.

g. ____________________ Our nations have much in common. We are both interested in progress for our people and in peace for all time. I sincerely hope your visit with us will be marked by the friendliness and candor that have been a hallmark of our past encounters.

h. ____________________ Before I bang the gavel for the last time, I wish to close my brief remarks with a sincerely felt "thank-you" for your support. If you give the same encouragement to Tom as you have given to me, his year in office will be a pleasant and rewarding one.

i. ____________________ As we gather to pay tribute to those who have fallen, let us remember that the storm clouds of war are ever approaching. We cannot relax our vigilance, lest we repeat more of these "days of memories" in future years.

j. ____________________ When Lincoln remarked, "The world will little note nor long remember what we do here," he was not thinking of this, the annual meeting of the Confectionary Sugar Union's convention. You need not be troubled, however, as the work that is carried on here will be significant, will be remembered by those who are benefactors of your decisions—the union members you represent.

UTILIZATION

4. Excerpts from speeches typifying five of the ceremonial types are presented below. Analyze the manner in which the excerpt satisfies the ceremonial function it represents.
   a. *Acceptance.* On January 10, 1951, President Harry S. Truman received the first Wilson award from the Woodrow Wilson Foundation. Excerpts from his acceptance speech follow:

   > I am grateful for the honor that the Woodrow Wilson Foundation has conferred upon me. . . . While I am honored to accept this award, I do so not in my name but in the name of the people of the United States. It is their award, it is they who have made this decision, that while peace is precious to us, freedom and justice are more precious. . . . To receive an honor like this from a foundation dedicated to him [Wilson] is about the highest honor that any man can achieve.[12]

   b. *Dedication.* On February 3, 1951, President Truman delivered an address dedicating the "Chapel of the Four Chaplains" in Philadelphia. Truman spoke of the faith of the chaplains, the unity this nation derives from faith, and the role of the U.S. in combatting efforts to destroy freedom, especially in regard to our involvement in Korea. The excerpt is printed below.

   > This chapel commemorates something more than an act of bravery or courage. . . . The four chaplains whose memory this chapel was built to commemorate were not required to give their lives as they did. They gave their lives without being asked.[13]

   c. *Presentation.* On January 30, 1951, Representative Sam Rayburn, Speaker of the House, was honored for his record service in the House, having just served longer than Henry Clay's $3056\frac{1}{2}$ days as speaker. President Truman delivered this presentation address:

I have a very pleasant duty to perform this morning to congratulate the Speaker of the House of Representatives on having served longer as Speaker of the House than any other man in the history of this Republic. And in order to show him that I feel very kindly toward him . . . I had a gavel made of wood from the White House that was used in 1817 to rebuild the White House after the British burned it.

But this is to Sam Rayburn who has served . . . with honor and devotion to his country, date January 10, 1951, and it is signed by the president.[14]

d. *Welcome.* In this excerpt, President Truman responded to a toast delivered by the President of Ecuador at a state dinner. Truman went on to note his wish to visit Ecuador and emphasized his familiarity with its capitol, Quitos. The excerpt is printed below.

I hope, Mr. President, that you will have a most pleasant visit all over these United States. I know you will have a cordial welcome wherever you go. They can't do anything else but give you a cordial welcome, because they are interested—all citizens of this country—in the welfare of the whole hemisphere, and I am sure, of the whole world. It is a pleasure to me to be your host and the representative of the 150 million citizens of the United States of America.[15]

e. *Commencement.* Harris Parker, Professor of Religion at Columbia College, Georgia, delivered that college's commencement address in August, 1974. The excerpt printed below outlines the principal themes Professor Parker developed in his address:

To paraphrase the tough-talking sheriff in a popular TV commercial, "American colleges are in a heap of trouble." It is not just financial trouble, although finances are part of the problem. Nor does the difficulty stem solely from a dwindling supply of potential students. The problem is much deeper and more profound: The American college has lost its way. Once it had a clear sense of mission, knew precisely what it was about, why it was here, what it was to do. Those days are gone now. Ambiguities prevail in place of certainty; the sense of mission dims; and the college, like a sleeping giant, waits for a summons to new life. I propose that we issue now such a summons.

The first task at hand is to re-discover a sense of purpose. It is to ask and to answer the question "Why are we here?" The second task is one of implementation—to set our house in order for the reasonable attainment of our goals, to make whatever modifications are necessary in the program and structure of the college in order to fulfill our purpose. But what, precisely, is this purpose? [16]

UTILIZATION

5. For each of the three situational descriptions that follow, construct a description of a rhetorical strategy you would employ.
   a. You are an assistant professor whose contract has not been renewed by the administration of your small, liberal arts college. You are well liked by the students and are invited to give a farewell speech at the Senior Honors Ceremony. You share the speaker's platform with the president of the college and with the dean, both of whom were instrumental in the nonrenewal of your contract. You have accepted a position for next year at a major university.
   b. You have been chosen as commencement speaker at the community college that you have attended for two years. The commencement ceremony is to be attended by the board of directors of the college, by the mayor and council members of the city in which your college is located, and by the governor (who also is speaking). Legislators from the state government also will be in attendance. In addition, the ceremony will be attended by the ordinary participants in such a ceremony—students, parents, and friends. You have enjoyed your two years at the college (the first two years of its existence) and feel that you have learned a great deal. You are deeply concerned that financial support for your institution, by both city and state agencies, is inadequate. Your campus needs an additional building and new staff members if it is to maintain instructional excellence. The governor has been quoted as saying, "We should put our chips on the four year universities of our state."
   c. You are the new president of a small manufacturing company. Your predecessor, who was removed from office because he lacked "fresh" ideas, has decided to retire at age 55 rather than suffer the humiliation of a lesser job with the company. As president of the company, you are expected to present an award to him for thirty years of service to the firm. You know that he feels betrayed by the firm and that members of the audience (fellow workers) are divided in loyalties between you and the former president.

The Means of Ceremonial Speaking

In the previous section, consideration was given to ten types of speeches that affirm values in ceremonial settings. In this section, attention will be given to the rhetorical means through which such speeches are accomplished. You already possess all of the areas of competence necessary for the successful preparation and presentation of speeches of this type. Thus, this section will merely focus your attention on the dimensions of rhetorical choice as they relate to the process of ceremonial speaking. Six guidelines will be provided.

Analyze the Ceremonial Requirements of the Situation

Throughout this book, it has been noted that audiences have expectations that may not be ignored. On ceremonial occasions, these expectations are especially well defined. If a speaker is to succeed, he or she must ensure that the address delivered is consistent with audience expectations. For example, when one attends a dedication ceremony one expects that the speaker will praise both the sacrifice of those who created the object being dedicated and the value of the object itself. When one attends a commencement speech, one expects that the graduates will be suitably honored and advised.

The speaker must begin preparation by analyzing audience expectations. When speakers misinterpret the ceremonial requirements of the occasion, it is unlikely that they will find success.

Choose Values Worthy of Praise or Blame

Speeches given on ceremonial occasions seek to strengthen the values held by members of the group addressed. Clearly the speaker must choose for praise or blame values that are consistent with the value structure of the audience addressed. In his "Farewell to the Cadets" speech, General MacArthur chose to praise duty, honor, and country as the values most to be cherished by military officers. Martin Luther King, Jr. in "I Have a Dream" chose to praise the values of creative suffering and nonviolent resistance—values that had governed the lives of many of those assembled.

As you prepare your ceremonial speech, give careful thought to the values that you will praise or blame. The values you choose may differ substantially from one audience to another. Were you to eulogize Harry Truman at a memorial service sponsored by the American Legion, you might choose to praise his patriotism, his dedication to national strength, and his disdain for totalitarian states. However, were you to eulogize Truman at a memorial service sponsored by a farm organization, you might choose to praise his dedication to rural America, his concern for the free and independent spirit, and his belief in soil and toil. In choosing values, you dare not violate the value structure of the audience addressed. In speeches of this type, you may be called upon to walk a very narrow line between the audience's values and your own personal sense of integrity.

Give Compelling Expression to Values through Organization

The organizational structure introduced in chapter 4 and affirmed in chapters 5 and 6, experiences stress as it is applied to speeches on ceremonial occasions. On many such occasions, statements of subject or purpose and a summary seem unnecessarily redundant. Although a ceremonial speech must be characterized by organizational integrity, the shape of the ideas presented is often strongly influenced by the ceremonial purpose served and the emotional climate which is present at that moment of public ceremony. For example, in a speech entitled "An Instrument of Revelation," Elizabeth Langer structured her eulogy to Arturo Toscanini in the following way: She began by noting the importance of music to humankind; then she described the final concert of the beloved maestro as his strength failed him; she then reviewed the major events of the maestro's life as he grew from a precocious child to an internationally renowned artist; she then described the qualities of the man that characterized his excellence as a musician and as a person and concluded by referring to the impact of his death on the world of music.[17]

As you organize your ceremonial speech, you must weigh the requirements of the ceremonial occasion against the traditional demands of organizational precision. Speeches of this type require your creative involvement in the ordering of ideas for their greatest emotional impact.

Give Compelling Expression to Values through Language

Ceremonial speeches, more than any other speech form, are characterized by vividness in language usage. Some of the most memorable moments of rhetorical excellence have occurred in speeches of this type: "The only thing we have to fear is fear itself"; "An iron curtain has descended"; "Ask not what your country can do for you—ask what you can do for your country"; and "I have a dream."

Since ceremonial speeches consider established values, the speaker must use vivid and stimulating language to give otherwise trite themes new life. Chapter 3 considered tactics of word choice, figurative use of language, and stylistic strategies for arranging ideas. All of these elements of language usage are relevant as you prepare your ceremonial speeches.

Give Compelling Expression to Values through Expository Materials

In chapter 5, the means of exposition were considered in the context of informative speeches. The devices considered there are equally relevant to speeches delivered on ceremonial occasions.

Vivid language without expository materials may seem empty. For generations, high school speakers in American Legion Oratorical Contests have spoken in hollow phrases in tribute to "democracy." While vivid language is important in ceremonial speeches, without the concreteness and specificity of expository materials it lacks precision and force. The effective combination of language and exposition was demonstrated by Elizabeth Langer as she underscored the role of principle in the life of Toscanini.

> But combined with this genius for interpretation and the perseverence necessary to develop this genius, Toscanini was a man of great principle. The Maestro hated dictatorship with a fiery passion. He defended the right and condemned the wrong regardless of the consequences. Once while playing a concert in Italy, he was ordered to stop and play "Giovenezza," the Fascist hymn to Mussolini. He turned to Mussolini's soldiers in the Concert Hall and said, "No, 'Giovenezza' is not music." For this defiant action in accordance with his principles, he was later beaten by the Fascists.[18]

The use of vivid language, combined with the use of striking example, enabled Langer to give strength to the value of "principle" in human life.

Give Compelling Expression to Values through Delivery

Different ceremonial occasions demand different kinds of delivery behaviors. It is expected that a political keynote address will be delivered in a vigorous and dynamic way. Eulogies and farewell addresses call for quiet, restrained vocal and physical behavior. Allen, Parish, and Mortensen provided two examples that stress the importance of using delivery behaviors that are appropriate to the occasion.

In 1962, in the eighty-second year of his life, General Douglas MacArthur returned to the United States Military Academy to receive the Sylvanus Thayer award for service to his nation. Despite failing health, the old soldier made a moving and inspirational address to the cadets. He talked of the values of duty, honor, and country—the motto inscribed on the academy coat of arms. He used no text or notes and spoke with little overt physical behavior. General MacArthur spoke in an exceptionally slow and deliberate manner. His rate was less than half of that of many speakers. His inflectional patterns lacked variety. Once gifted with a rich and resonant voice, his voice now seemed hoarse and at times faint. Yet, his speech was an outstanding success. Why? His delivery seemed appropriate to the man, to the mood of his farewell message, and to the occasion.

The second example took place on January 20, 1961. Speaking to a large outdoor audience before the nation's capitol on a cold, clear day, John Fitzgerald Kennedy delivered his Presidential Inaugural Address. In contrast to his rapid-fire campaign delivery, Kennedy spoke at a medium rate giving careful emphasis to his ideas. His manner of delivery was vigorous although restrained. His message was communicated with vocal intensity. His physical behavior, abundant on the campaign trail, was restrained. Why were Kennedy's vocal and physical behaviors so different from his campaign delivery strategies? The occasion seemed to demand it. A President is more than a barnstorming politician. An inaugural ceremony is vested with more dignity than a political rally. An inaugural audience expects delivery behavior different from campaign speaking.[19]

You must ensure that your delivery of ceremonial speeches is consistent with audience expectations.

One additional caution is in order regarding the delivery of speeches on ceremonial occasions. Because such speeches are designed to give compelling expression to ideas, speakers often prepare a complete manuscript from which they read their messages. Since the reading of manuscripts poses special problems, speakers should exercise additional care in preparation. They should not seem buried in their notes. They should not appear restricted in their physical behavior. They should not sound like readers rather than speakers. To avoid these problems, carefully consider the physical circumstances in which the address will be read. Will a stiff wind blow the pages away? Will reduced sources of lighting make the manuscript difficult to see? Having considered these circumstances, practice to make the words on the printed page sound spontaneous and natural.

EXERCISES

VERIFICATION

6. List the six guidelines for ceremonial speaking.

VERIFICATION

7. Identify the brief descriptions of guidelines below by using the following key phrases: analyze requirements; choose values; organization; language; expository materials; delivery.

   a. ________________ Arrange themes according to the ceremonial purpose.

   b. ________________ Use of dynamic or restrained presentation.

   c. ________________ Use concrete details in supporting theme.

   d. ________________ Appropriate use of style to attain vivid and clear statement of theme.

   e. ________________ Analyze the audience expectations.

   f. ________________ Choose appropriate themes.

UTILIZATION

8. Identify the guidelines being violated in the following descriptions of rhetorical events. Use the key phrases listed in exercise 7. If none is violated, write "none" in the space provided.

   a. ________________ A speaker employs a vigorous, denunciatory tone during a eulogy to a departed leader.

b. ______________________ A speaker vilifies America as an imperialistic nation whose soldiers have died while fighting abroad. This speech is delivered to the American Legion on Memorial Day.

c. ______________________ A speaker highlights the theme of a convention in a vivid, memorable style.

d. ______________________ A speech is well delivered, beautifully expressed, but devoid of substance.

e. ______________________ A speaker stresses the stubbornness and stinginess of the departed millionaire.

f. ______________________ A speaker follows a careful statement of purpose with a partition of subjects during his acceptance speech.

g. ______________________ A speaker uses a colloquial style in welcoming the Queen of England to our shores.

Preparing Your Ceremonial Speech

In this section, we will present a ceremonial speech evaluation form based on the guidelines discussed in the previous section. Two speeches will then be provided for your analysis.

Ceremonial Speech Evaluation Form	Comments
Speech Structure	
Introduction	
Organizational Integrity	
Conclusion	
Transitions	
Use of Language	
Word Choice	
Figures of Speech	
Stylistic Arrangement of Ideas	

Use of Expository Devices
Kinds Used
Effectiveness

Delivery
Vocal Aspects
Physical Aspects

Overall Ceremonial Effect
Values Focused Upon
Appropriateness of Values to Audience

A Speech of Commemoration: San Francisco
By Catherine Mayer

1. She is a magical lady. Ever enchanting, ever changing, she holds her friends enthralled with a spirit mysterious that sparkles, and dances, and mourns, and somehow matches our mood, or perhaps makes it, more than we know.

2. She is a city of high buildings, and fishing boats, and old men playing evening checkers in old Portsmouth Square. She is the city of Coit Tower, Ferlinghetti's City Lights Bookstore, and fiery Chinese dragons weaving and breathing in the Year of the Rooster.

3. She is San Francisco, matchless and maverick. In a riot of hills and a spindrift of salt spray, she catches us up and casts her spell, gently leading us as her mood will.

4. Today she is merry! Kites roam wildly on the ocean breeze, above the old windmill, out in Golden Gate Park. The ferry to Tiburon is churning up white froth, through sunlit sparkles of water, with seagulls crying and circling above. The cable car has stopped at the neighborhood's creamiest ice cream parlor, before clanging down the Hyde Street hill toward the Ships Museum and the blue bay. And down in Union Square, the pigeons have never been so comical in earning their daily oddments. Cascades of mums and violets, tulips, baby's breath, daisies and daffodils tumble from Jake's flower stand outside I. Magnin's. And the enchantment of a Vivaldi concerto filters through the crowds of noon shoppers, offered by the young, long-haired musicians on the corner where Doubleday sells its posters and paperbacks.

5. But it often happens that on a cool, clear day, San Francisco seems more sedate and sophisticated. Her mood is magnanimous rather than frolicsome and whimsical. Her bridges arch serenely over silver currents and full-sailed schooners running with the wind. The views from penthouses and tiny, wooden garrets alike, quicken the breath, and offer, at one glance, to the imagination, not just sight, but all smells, sounds, and histories. The fashionable bars on Union Street fill up with elegant and eligible young women and men from the financial district, and the Sea

Witch and the Wine Cellar at Ghirardelli Square begin early serving Irish Coffee and hot mulled wine. In her magnanimity, San Francisco offers atmosphere and cuisine for the most particular. The Taj of India is elegant and spicy; the Call Board quiet and intimate. And at Sam Wo's, the old Confucian waiter on the third floor will holler after you and thrust a full teapot, three bowls of rice, and bunches of chopsticks into your hands as you stagger through the noisy kitchen toward a table. Elegant or egalitarian. It is all there. She won't let you down.

6. Ah, but I have known her, too, when her mood is melancholy. The fog drifts slowly, swinging around the street lamps, muffling two scuffling alley cats, and slipping between silent, mossy trees on the pathway going up Telegraph Hill. Masts loom suddenly out of the misty grayness down at the marina, boats rocking eerily and creaking amongst themselves. The red lights on the top span of the Golden Gate Bridge blink momentarily before the gliding fog reclaims the patch of night sky. And the foghorn on the rocks out along the coast moans its lonely warning, and moans again.

7. Like any of us, San Francisco has many moods. But whether she is merry or magnanimous or melancholy, there is a special beauty about her—as though she carries a magic lantern, whose light imparts a wonder, a sparkle, a vitality to every rivulet of fog, to every circling gull.[20]

A Eulogy: An Instrument of Revelation

By Elizabeth Langer

1. Time has a way of preserving forever the meaningful creations in the Universe. Culture is the expression of the very best thoughts of Man inspired by God. And one of the most beloved forms of culture is music.

2. Some men love music for the images it creates. Through music, some soar happily through space. Music to some brings back childhood faith and dreams. And to others it represents the closeness of God.

3. But however music strikes him, man needs music for fulfillment and for life.

4. To be alive is not merely to exist. All people exist; but few really live. A living man is one imbued with a spiritual vitality channeled towards the really meaningful aspects of life. Thus it seems fitting to make a humble plea that you might never forget one who not merely existed, but lived.

5. Arturo Toscanini led his farewell concert on April 4, 1954. Carnegie Hall overflowed with his admirers and his life-long friends. As the lights began to dim, a dignified man walked slowly to his earned position at the center of the stage. He was short of stature, but walked with a confidence reminiscent of a once bursting energy. His long-flowing white hair, deepset moist eyes, expressive thin fingers, suggested the lovable quality of the true artist. His manner was serene and unpretentious. Throughout the performance of Wagner, one of the Maestro's favorite composers, a loving audience wept shamelessly as it watched the quality of the Maestro's work deteriorate before its eyes. His strength was gone, and he had no heart

for his music. A few times he gripped a nearby rail for support. And the concert ended with Toscanini only beating time. He had once said to his close friends, probably those in the audience at that very moment, "When the baton trembles in my hand, I shall conduct no more." The baton did tremble that night, and Arturo Toscanini never conducted again. And on January 17 of this year, the great Maestro died at fourscore and nine.

6. What of the origins of this man whom we honor today? Arturo Toscanini was born in Parma. As a child he studied at the Conservatory. At the age of nineteen he had earned the colossal title of Maestro by performing the incredible task of conducting the opera *Aida* from memory. At thirty-one, the boyhood dreams and aspirations of one who was destined to become the greatest musical genius of our age were realized when he lifted his baton to conduct at La Scala in Milan, the highest culmination to which any musician can aspire in Italy. In 1907 Toscanini came to the Metropolitan Opera House, where for seven years he thrilled music patrons. In the later '20s he toured the United States, bringing beauty and happiness to the lives of millions who needed inspiration during the disastrous depression. And in 1937, he conducted the first of his concerts with the NBC Symphony in Radio City. Here, through the miracle of radio, the electrifying music of Arturo Toscanini was heard and appreciated by the poor as well as by the rich.

7. During this preparation, Toscanini sought always the meaning of his life. But discovering this meaning was for him only the beginning. Bringing beauty and inspiration to the lives of all men was his mission.

8. The Maestro was an indefatigable and even a fanatical perfectionist. To watch him conduct was to experience his joy in carefully interpreting the score as the composer visioned it and the joy coming from his unbounded love for good music.

9. There were those of small discernment who thought of him as a tyrant. There were those who placed undue emphasis upon the extravagance of his manner. Had the Maestro disciplined his musicians for personal attainment, he might justifiably have been called a tyrant. But the reason for his uncompromising methods was one of humility. The Maestro believed that the revelation of the composer's intent was the musician's sole reason for being. His personal integrity required him honestly to recreate with his orchestra the composer's meaning. The composer was his master and his disciplinarian.

10. The interpretative genius does not owe success to inspiration alone. With it goes the painstaking effort to learn and to be an instrument of revelation. And how well the Maestro had mastered this rule. Not once in 70 years of conducting did he approach the platform with a musical score. For every concert he memorized every work. He once said, "The conductor should have the score in his head, rather than his head in the score." Was he not a humble servant of the composer?

11. But combined with this genius for interpretation and the perseverence necessary to develop this genius, Toscanini was a man of great principle. The Maestro hated dictatorship with a fiery passion. He defended the right and condemned the wrong regardless of the consequences. Once while

playing a concert in Italy, he was ordered to stop and play "Giovenezza," the Fascist hymn to Mussolini. He turned to Mussolini's soldiers in the Concert Hall and said, "No, 'Giovenezza' is not music." For this defiant action in accordance with his principles, he was later beaten by the Fascists.

12. Dorothy Gordon once wrote that "Toscanini's whole musical life has been one uncompromising fight against usurpation." And how true this is. The Maestro fought constantly against the usurpation by the conductor of the composer's real meaning. He fought against the usurpation of any single instrument in his orchestra. To Toscanini a work of art was a harmonious entity where no usurpation could exist.

13. But just as Arturo Toscanini was a strong, masterful, uncompromising genius, he did not seek adulation. The Maestro was not a sensational music maker because he would not allow himself to become sensational. Many an audience in Carnegie Hall has seen him leave the stage in the midst of a tumultuous applause. He possessed the serenity and the devotion of the true artist, and pretentions were foreign to him.

14. The January 17 issue of the New York Times carried the headline, "Arturo Toscanini is dead." Newspaper boys shouted from the street-corners of Milan, "The Maestro is dead." The NBC Symphony in Radio City gave a concert in his honor—the Maestro is dead. La Scala in Milan was closed down, and a special mass was said in St. Peter's—the Maestro is dead. But death is such a final term to apply here. For Arturo Toscanini was more than an existing organism. He was a living man, alive in his music. Music was Toscanini, and death killed him only physically. The greatest part of Arturo Toscanini will live on as long as man occupies a position on the universe.

15. Several years ago, Lawrence Gilman paid a tribute to the Maestro which I pray will never be forgotten:

> Arturo Toscanini is among the foremost prophets of that subliminal world of indestructible beauty and reality. He is no visionary who has merely slept and dreamed there. He is creatively alive there—an active *instrument of revelation.*[21]

EXERCISES

UTILIZATION

9. Analyze the preceding speeches using the ceremonial speech evaluation form. You may omit the section on delivery. All other categories should be completed.

UTILIZATION

10. Prepare and deliver a four to five minute ceremonial speech that meets the criteria of the evaluation form. Eulogies and commemorative speeches are especially recommended.

Notes

1. Chaim Perelman and L. Olbrechts-Tyteca, *The New Rhetoric: A Treatise on Argumentation,* trans. John Wilkinson and Purcell Weaver (Notre Dame, Indiana: University of Notre Dame Press, 1969), p. 51.

2. Ibid., p. 53.

3. Douglas MacArthur, "Farewell to the Cadets," in Wil A. Linkugel, R. R. Allen, and Richard L. Johannesen, *Contemporary American Speeches,* 3d ed. (Belmont, California: Wadsworth, 1972), p. 285.

4. Adlai Stevenson, "The Educated Citizen," in *What I Think,* by Adlai Stevenson (New York: Harper and Row, 1956), pp. 172–74.

5. John F. Kennedy, "Ich Bin Ein Berliner," *Public Papers of the Presidents: John F. Kennedy, 1963* (Washington, D.C.: Government Printing Office, 1964), pp. 524–25.

6. Edward M. Kennedy, "Eulogy to Robert F. Kennedy," *New York Times,* 9 June 1968, p. 56.

7. Abraham Lincoln, "Farewell Address at Springfield," in *Letters and Addresses of President Lincoln* (New York: Unit Book Publishing Co., 1905), pp. 181–182.

8. John F. Kennedy, "Inaugural Address," Linkugel et al., *American Speeches* 3d ed., pp. 296–299.

9. Joseph T. Ling, "Research: Key to Quality Water Service in the '80s," in *Vital Speeches* 41 (1 August 1975): 616.

10. Harry S. Truman, *Public Papers of the Presidents, 1951* (Washington, D.C.: Government Printing Office, 1965), p. 200.

11. Ibid., p. 342–43.

12. Ibid., p. 17–18.

13. Ibid., p. 139.

14. Ibid., p. 128.

15. Ibid., p. 355.

16. Harris Parker, "In Pursuit of Purpose," *Vital Speeches* 30 (15 September 1974): 729.

17. Elizabeth Langer, "An Instrument of Revelation," in Linkugel et al., *American Speeches,* 3d ed., pp. 300–303.

18. Ibid., p. 302.

19. R. R. Allen, Sharol Parish, and C. David Mortensen, *Communication: Interacting through Speech* (Columbus, Ohio: Charles E. Merrill Publishing Company, 1974), pp. 404–405.

20. Catherine Mayer, Unpublished Manuscript, University of Wisconsin, 1973.

21. Elizabeth Langer, "An Instrument of Revelation," in Linkugel et al., *American Speeches,* 3d ed., pp. 300–303.

Index